THE
BOOK
OF
PANDAS

By Kimberly M. Tsan
Illustrations by Celia Libelle

Table of Contents

Once Upon a Panda

THE DECK ORIGIN STORY

While "utter cuteness" for me is enough of a reason to create a panda-themed deck, I created this deck because I wanted to capture the sweet, playful, introspective, and carefree nature of the panda spirit through the archetypes of tarot. I find panda's affectionate and happy-go-lucky energy perfectly suited for the intuitive and psychospiritual nature of contemporary tarot practice - they're innocently heartwarming and at the same time adorably wise when it comes to keeping things simple and being in the moment.

"What do you mean I'm wise? I'm just a panda!" is what I imagine pandas will say if you ever want to thank them for your cathartic moments. According to them, all they did was roll around and munch on bamboos all day. This is one of the biggest reasons why I adore pandas and adore working with the energy of pandas – they don't seem to take life that seriously, and they have this "cute but savage" confidence. I don't know if you know, pandas *love* practical jokes. Panda mothers frequently use their sizable paws to keep eager cubs at bay to prevent them from stealing their bamboos, hogging their snacks to themselves as they shamelessly declare some me-time. I also saw video footage once of a panda casually tipping a fellow panda over off a short bridge into a ditch – and then quickly walking off as if it had nothing to do with him.

I laughed so hard I think I must have produced abs: six-pack abs, a solid board of steel. I found it funny because…*pandas are pandas.* They're just so…*themselves.* They don't see themselves as anything more than their adorable panda selves. They don't know that they're endangered. They don't know that we are doing our best to make sure pandas swipe right on panda Tinder to eventually get some "action" on. They don't know that they are often associated with Eastern philosophy, and they don't know that they're important.

I don't know. I just find the contrast rather amusing. These black and white bears are so imbued with meaning, yet they are just so…obviously unaware! I mean, I suppose you could argue the same for animal archetypes in general. Do animal spirits intend to become archetypes or are they just embodiments of our ideas that we project unto them? That's a long discussion and a story to be told at another time, but I mention it because a lot of animal totems do carry an air of wisdom about them: the lions for their prowess and rulership, the deer for their softness and tenderness, and the elephant for their ancient sight and grounding nature. Meanwhile, pandas are wiggling their butts against a piece of wood and doing some crazy sideway twerking in order to scratch an itch.

Each animal archetype carries its own unique wisdom – there is no doubt about that. But in my mind, pandas are especially interesting because their wisdom is so unalarming and often so unexpected. They have the eternal charm and joy of a child, as well as the ease and depth of a wise sage. The fact that they happen to inspire us with their presence seems like a happy accident, and pandas will never claim to be wise. They will simply claim to be pandas and proceed to behave like one. And in a way, in the uh, *panda way*, or *way of the panda* – I think that is the perfect philosophy for living life. Life isn't something you need to claim or proclaim. Life is about being in the moment. There is nothing you can really claim in life other than the moment you are in right now.

So live in that moment. Like a panda running and unraveling baskets of dry leaves that their nannies have so desperately trying to sweep, or climbing on top of each other and wrestling to pull each other's ear off with their teeth. Pandas are precious. Just like life is precious. Life is sweet, wonderful, adorable – and so are you. You're precious beyond measure. You're a story that unwraps itself like a present – an experience, a moment that unfolds, and (quoting Rumi) *an entire universe in ecstatic motion.*

There is no boundary to your existence, no limits. You can do whatever you want at any given moment. Each moment of *you* is a moment of joy that never ceases. So be free. Live without worry and regret. Expand and roll into every moment with furry panda pizzazz.

How to Use This Book

In your hands, you are holding the official guidebook to the Way of the Panda Tarot. This book is interactive, story and character-driven, and full of lighthearted humor that frequently involves the breaking of the fourth wall as well as panda vs author banters. The pandas are very chatty (especially the Suit of Swords – this humble author had to wrestle for her keyboard while she was writing that chapter) and they are all very eager to lend you their paws to assist you on your tarot journey.

The Book of Pandas launches straight into the world of pandas. You will learn about pandas as archetypes and animal totems, and you will also learn about how you can tap into their spirit, their strengths and their wisdom to live an empowered, peaceful and pandatastic life. After figuring out where you land on the panda spectrum, the book will lead you to meet the Major Pandas, the Elemental Pandas, and the Panda Courts.

The symbolism and traditional meanings of tarot are fused and combined with the wisdom from the panda archetype – as well as stories from the Panda Kingdom.

If you're a total tarot newbie, the pandas want to tell you that they are incredibly honored and happy that the Panda Kingdom is the very first place you shall visit. They hope you will return often to spend time with them, and perhaps bring them tales of your other adventures outside of the Panda Kingdom as you explore the rest of the tarot world. But just a heads-up – if you wish to study the system of tarot in-depth, you may want to look for alternative guidebooks or additional resources to supplement your endeavor to build a firm foundation of tarot. While this book offers you plenty of information on each tarot card and their meanings, it doesn't really follow the typical structure of a tarot guidebook. You won't be seeing keywords, upright meanings and reversed meanings here – the Little Black & White Book (Book of Panda's little brother) will be perfect for a bite-sized tarot crash course and quick references.

As you journey through this book, you'll see that each section of tarot has a little something different to offer. The Major Pandas invite you to connect with the archetypal wisdom of each Major Arcana – giving you instructions and insights on how to "summon" a Major Panda's Panda Power to transform your worldview and your own life. The Elemental Pandas, or the Minor Arcana, will focus on raising your awareness and inspiring you to make better and empowering decisions, as well as encouraging you to perceive both challenges and blessings as portals of opportunity through whimsical tales and adorable panda fables. Last but not least, the Court Cards are where the Royal Pandas introduce themselves to you – they will share with you their motivations, their strengths, and their flaws so you can recognize situations where you may need to step into their character roles to make the best of any situation.

Though each section kind of took a life of its own – they are all written with the same intention in mind: to help you access and maximize your panda power. To comfort you when you're stuck and trapped in dark, unreachable places. To supercharge you to not bypass any challenge, but to view them as opportunities for growth. During such moments, you can expect to see an army of pandas – who will always lend you their paws, who will help you take down the monsters in your psyche with their legendary bamboo staff and adorable kung fu moves, who will hug you with all the love that they have and who will always, always, *always*, believe in you and all that you do – show up to support you as you walk the Way of the Panda.

How Much of a Panda Are You?

KNOW THY PANDA SELF

The following quiz will help you identify your panda tendencies and determine your panda percentage. Let us explore to see if you have a strong inner panda dwelling within your fibers! Wherever you are on the panda spectrum, knowing the extent of you panda-ness can help you gain insight to how you approach and relate to the world and shed light on how you can best tap into the strength of the panda archetype and navigate your panda tendencies to continue to level up in life.

There are 25 statements in the following quiz, and to determine your panda-ness, rate each statement from 0 – 4. When you are done, add up all the numbers to find out your panda score!

SCORING GUIDE

☼ 0 being "this statement is totally not me / does not describe me / nuh-uh"

☼ 1 being "very rarely / not enough to call it a trait or form a pattern"

☼ 2 being "I guess? sometimes I do this / not all the time / depends"

☼ 3 being "yup, I do this often / pretty much yeah / I agree"

☼ 4 being "omg this is 100% me / YAAAS / get out of my head"

The Panda Personality Quiz

1. ____ You identify yourself as an introvert
2. ____ You are nonconfrontational and do not like conflicts
3. ____ You are shy at first but once you get to know someone, you're a total goofball
4. ____ You find it a bit awkward to be in the center of attention
5. ____ You are playful when it comes to the people you love and care about

6. ____ People often describe you as sweet, cute, and adorable
7. ____ There is a wise and "deep" part of you that tends to surprise people
8. ____ You don't like excessive displays of affection but like to cozy-snuggle
9. ____ You don't feel the need to assert your confidence just to prove a point
10. ____ You value mutual respect, honesty, and humility

11. ____ You're more of a listener than a talker
12. ____ You like going with the flow and keeping the peace
13. ____ You would describe yourself as down to earth and a "chill" person
14. ____ You like to spend time with your thoughts and figuring things out on your own
15. ____ You're not particularly outdoorsy or sporty

16. ___ You have a vivid imagination and a colorful inner world
17. ___ You have simple tastes and interests (not minimalistic, but nothing fancy)
18. ___ You always order the same thing (your favourite dish) when you go to a restaurant
19. ___ You find comfort and joy in the things you already know
20. ___ You are very connected to your inner child

21. ___ You love being goofy / silly / quirky and you love people who do the same
22. ___ You wear your heart on your sleeve
23. ___ You are empathetic – with a special fondness to small creatures and pets
24. ___ You're not afraid to spend time alone (you relish it, in fact!)
25. ___ Sipping a cup of tea in silence, reading a book, and staring at the ceiling are rich, dynamic and fulfilling activities with lots of joy and texture

YOUR TOTAL SCORE

After using the calculator because I am incapable of mental math, I conclude that my total score is:

_____

Unlike the general public that is incapable of mental math, I conclude with my expert mathematic capabilities that my total score is:

_____

Your Panda-ness Revealed

Scored 0 – 25: You're as Cute as a Panda, but Not Much of a Panda

If you've gone through this quiz with little to no feelings of resonance, the panda archetype probably isn't strong in your personality. You might be someone who's more driven to explore and experience the world in more action-packed ways - you enjoy adventures that tire you physically, and you enjoy the buzz and the drums and loud music. Your "quiet moment" may not necessarily be holding a cup of tea while curling up in a blanket next to a fireplace - but that doesn't mean you don't know how to find your peace. One thing is for sure, though - even though you're not much of a panda inside, I'm pretty sure you're as cute as you can get, and nothing stops you from indulging in your love of pandas!

Scored 26 – 50: Part-Time Panda - You Clock in When You Need To

If you've scored in this range, you're a part-time panda and you're likely an ambivert - someone who can be introverted or extraverted depending on the situation! You enjoy simple quiet moments but you totally don't mind going out in the world to engage with people and seek new thrills. You may be constantly torn about keeping things simple or pursuing some refinement / something more exquisite – always swinging in between extremes. To you, it's always this balancing act of weighing your self-expression, your desires, your expectations, and your personal truths. You don't really mind the tug-o-war though - having some healthy tension pushes you to amalgamate and discover unique strengths in your personality that allow you to navigate both the calmer and faster currents of the world.

Scored 51 – 75: The Inner Panda is Strong with This One

You have a strong inner panda! While you know how to set and go at your own tempo, you sometimes struggle with the fast-paced demands of the world. Navigating complicated social situations could prove to be challenging for you. You're a gentle soul and a peace-loving person and ideally, you want everybody to get along! Because of this, balancing your need for social acceptance and personal boundaries can be a tricky business indeed. For the most part, you are incredibly loving, and you like to shower people with your affections with little gifts and simple gestures. Oh, and last but not least - while it is true that you are generally sweet-tempered, the people around you should really, *really,* learn to not touch your food. Especially your pizza.

Scored 76 – 100: You're a Panda in Human Skin

You are a panda - panda panda panda! Your worldview is simple, colorful and pure. You are less impressed by shiny things edged with gold - you value meaning, and the genuine expression of a moment. The others may often be fooled by your unalarming appearance but once they get to know you, they will discover the rich layers and textures within your personality and be impressed by your depth and your inner child sage. You are likable, carefree, lighthearted, and you always live in the moment. Little things bring you immense joy - and you are always grateful for the blessings that you have in life. With a heart as big and tender as yours, you go about life with optimism, adorable wisdom and ease. Oh, and you're irrevocably cute.

PONDERING PANDA

☼ What's your favourite thing about pandas?
☼ Did you resonate with the quiz results? Why or why not? What was something that you learned about the panda archetype or about yourself?
☼ When do you think will be a useful moment to call on your inner panda?
☼ How do you picture strength and confidence? What kind of strength do you see in pandas? How is that similar or different from what you have in mind?

Panda Spreads for Pandas of All Levels

If You're as Cute as a Panda, but Not Much of a Panda: Even though you're not much of a panda, the pandas will still like to support you and shower you with their love! Here is a spread to help you channel some panda if you ever need them:

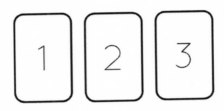

1. What best illustrates your relationship with the panda archetype?
2. How does the panda archetype benefit you and what power can it offer?
3. How can you keep doing you?

If You're a Part-Time Panda – You Clock in When You Need To: Alright part-time panda! Let's see how the pandas can help you balance this very intricate dance of occasional panda-ing.

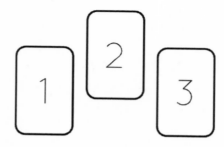

1. When is the best time for you to "clock in" on panda mode?
2. When is the best time for you to shift gears and tap into different energies?
3. How can you carry the panda spirit and live a carefree life full of joy and ease?

The Inner Panda Energy is Strong with This One: People with strong inner pandas often find themselves needing to navigate the fast-paced demands of the world around them. Here is a spread for you when you're asking the age-old question: to panda or not to panda? Ah, that is the question.

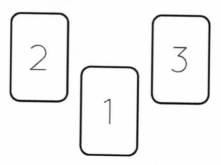

1. How can you channel your inner panda and play tai chi with the fast-paced demands of the world?

2.   What can you do when you feel pressured towards conflicting social needs?

3.   How can you make peace with yourself when you don't know if you should panda or not?

If You're a Panda in Human Skin: Hurrah! Say no more, fellow Panda-Jedi. Your cosmic panda-ness must be properly harnessed and unleashed into the world to induce a necessary panda-monium. Here is a spread to help you do just that:

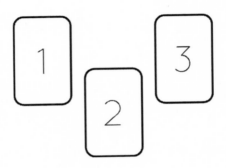

1.   How can you best let your inner panda roll out and shine?

2.   How can you unleash your incredible panda energy and expand your fluffy aura to consume – I mean, uh, to positively affect – everyone around you?

3.   What is a perspective that you normally don't consider that you can incorporate into your all too panda practice?

Entering the Panda Kingdom

AN INTERACTIVE TAROT JOURNEY

The pandas will like to officially welcome you and lead you to the fabled and legendary Panda Kingdom, and they insist on doing it properly. You will need your Way of the Panda Tarot deck for this exercise. Other than that, you don't need to bring anything else other than an open heart to enter the Land of the Pandas. The pandas do not discriminate – having that said, if it's not too much trouble for you – the pandas will never say no to yummy snacks or bamboo stalks. It may or may not hasten the entrance process.

As you read the following passage, visualize yourself embarking on the journey with the pandas. There is power in our imagination – it is the space where our intuition and creativity meet. It is the space of inner magic – the pandas advise you to use the powers of your imagination wisely, and at the right places.

BEGIN YOUR JOURNEY

Sit in a comfortable position and take a deep breath – have your Way of the Panda Tarot by your side. Relax your mind and body and open the gates of your imagination. If you want, you can picture yourself wearing a panda onesie, or something equally presentable.

You're about to enter the World of the Pandas. In your hand, a formal invitation written on hard slips of bamboo. The woody document has a chewed corner on it; the messenger must have been hungry and taken a bite. You can see that whoever delivered the bamboo slip took great care to gnaw around the text, cleverly preserving the writings while satiating the demands of their belly.

If this is your first time visiting the Panda Kingdom, there is no need to worry. You do not need to bring anything; you only need to bring yourself. The truth is, you don't even need to bring the invitation, as you are always welcome here in the World of Pandas.

A red panda is coming to you now – his bushy tail trailing and bouncing behind him like a striped winter scarf in the wind. He approaches you nimbly, with a friendly twitch of his whiskers. He is here to greet you, and he shall guide you to meet the lovely pandas – who are patiently waiting for food offerings – I mean, uh, for you. The red panda is excited to see you. From the way he stands up on his hind legs and the way his little beady eyes sparkle – you can tell how much love he has for you. For you! A total stranger in the Panda Lands! What have you done to deserve such adoration?

As if sensing your thoughts, the red panda answers. "The pandas can't wait to see you! You're causing quite a ruckus among the monochrome bears. They won't stop talking about how awesome you are and how much they love you already. The pandas are stoked!"

"But we haven't even met!" you exclaim, touched by the sentiment. "How could they love me already?"

"Because you're lovely," the red panda twitches his nose. "Because you are who you are without question, and you are exactly who you need to be at this very moment."

PAUSE

From your deck, shuffle and pull out a panda card. This card will represent what pandas already love about you at this very moment. What makes you lovely? What makes you who you are?

"Awww," you can't help but say.

"Come now!" The red panda grabs your hand. "The pandas are all waiting for you! It's going to be MAJOR, let me tell ya!" The red panda chuckles. "Oh, by the way, here's your gift. The pandas insisted. It's sort of like a divine blessing, but pawed by a panda."

The red panda urges you to open the box. You accept it gingerly, and you begin to unwrap the golden bamboo leaves that encase the box.

You grin when you see that half of the leaves are chewed and snacked upon, leaving it in slight disarray and giving it a messy DIY beauty. What could it be?

PAUSE

From your deck, shuffle and pull out a panda card. This will be the Panda Blessing you shall receive from this journey. This is the gift that the pandas have given you, wrapped in their adorable love.

"Wow, this is awesome, thank you!" You say, and you hold the gift to your heart – flushing with gratitude and joy.

"Are you ready to meet the Major Pandas?" the red panda asks, jumping up and standing on his tiptoes, trying to grab you by the hand to lead the way. (In your imagination, you better be a good sport and bend down a little to allow this to happen!)

"Yes!"

"Of course you are. Let's go!"

And with the little red panda as your guide, you cross the threshold and set foot in the land of the pandas for the first time – or for the second time, or third. No matter how many times you visit, the pandas will greet you with the same love and excitement. Because you're you. And who could possibly be lovelier?

The Major Arcana

MAJOR PANDAS WITH SOME MAJOR WISDOM TO IMPART

The Major Pandas are the Guardians of the Panda Kingdom. They look after their fellow pandas and they show up whenever their transformative presence is needed. When they're not busy helping their fellow pandas, they visit mankind to help us make peace with our troubles and life shenanigans. They have a keen interest in lurking in the world of mankind and lending a paw to whoever that is in need of their special powers. In this chapter, you will meet the Major Pandas, and you learn about each of their unique panda magic and panda perspective when it comes to personal transformation and living life to the fullest.

The Fool

*Make a wish, or a thousand wishes, as you blow
out the candles of your Cosmic Birthday Cake.
The pandas are lighting sparklers and blowing
party horns all around you – they are excited to
send you off to your next big conquest. What will
you do? And how far will you go? As far as
dreams can reach, the pandas hope.*

The Fool is an adventurous panda that always lives in the
moment. His heart is an open field, a fresh canvas waiting for
colorful currents to rush in and tumble. The world is an
edgeless map, and there is always more to discover, to
experience, and to explore. As the day resets itself at dawn, The
Fool reaches for his trusty red pouch and strings it on a bamboo
stick. He always travels light, for the only things he needs to
enter the space of infinite potential are his passion and his
enthusiasm – and maybe some snacks. His loyal sidekick, Little
Red Panda, never leaves his side and follows him into exciting
new prologues as well as the many wild unknowns. Like the
panda, red pandas are also gentle spirits with great patience and
sensitivity. These two besties look out for each other as they set
out to conquer the world.

Panda Power Up

The Fool hands you his Panda Party Hat. This special hat (blessed with panda magic) links and rushes the currents of your soul directly to your feet, conveniently bypassing your fears, your conditioning, and your self-doubts. This way, when your soul hears the calling of an adventure, your feet will automatically spring to action – without restraint, and without excuses, and without hesitation! The Panda Party Hat also regularly sends celebratory vibes and excess adrenaline into your bloodstream, so that you are always pumped and ready to take the first steps to forever change your life. Wear it frequently and joyously – for it is a hat that can withstand any weather. The more you wear it, the brighter it becomes!

THE FOOL'S GUIDE TO CONQUERING THE WORLD

- ☼ Travel lightly – no baggage allowed!
- ☼ Sparkle with excitement (or if you're incapable of sparkling, you may grin from ear to ear)
- ☼ Find yourself a red panda, but guard your snacks and provisions
- ☼ Everything is going to be awesome!
- ☼ YOLO! You only live once. So live for once!

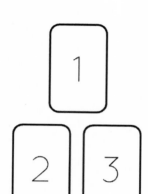

The Party Hat

1. You are invited – by the Universe. It's a party as long as you show up. How will you prepare for this new exciting venture?

2. The pandas are ready to launch you into the new world like a rocket! Where does your heart tell you to go?

3. The Red Panda will be your loyal sidekick. Although, be warned, he just might eat all your snacks when you're not looking. How will you be supported as you spread your panda wings and fly?

The Magician

Pandalf is looking through his spell-book. No, not the Compendium of Bamboozling Spells written by Esteemed Pandicorn Leafdancer. He's looking for the blank spell notebook – for writing spells, of course. You are his favourite guest, and to manifest your dreams and everything you've wanted, he plans to write a special spell, just for you.

Pandalf is always working. If he's not eating (which is most of the time) he is busy attempting to bring his big dreams to life. In his lair of alchemy and magic, you will see him squinting his eyes to extract correct measurements for the potion he's brewing or restructuring sentences and syllables to refine a spell. You may even see him planting, fertilizing and replotting his delicate herbs at all once. And on the days where he feels particularly fireproof, he will attempt to shoot out balls of flame from his paws – a very bold experiment for a panda with extremely flammable fur. The people and pandas that admire his work tend to think that he draws power from the hat that he wears, but he always laughs at the notion. He is Pandalf, the Panda of Many Magical Talents, and magic sparkles from his core and courses through his veins. His powers are inherent – not given by a silly hat.

Panda Power Up

What is it that you crave in life? Pandalf is very interested in knowing, because he intends to use every bit of his power to help you create the outcome that you desire – the life you've been dreaming of that you utterly deserve. With one paw, he scribbles furiously in his spell book, incorporating your desires, your dreams and visions along with your cosmic coordinates into his magic. With his other paw, he carefully places his much-coveted wizard hat on your head. It is not meant to be an instrument that gives you power. It is a token, to remind you of the world-altering powers that have nested within your being since the beginning of your existence. Your raw power and talents need constant use and nurture in order to grow and develop – and Pandalf suggests that you put on your magic hat and start now.

THE MAGICIAN'S GUIDE
TO CONQUERING THE WORLD

☼ Always write your own spells. It's more effective when they rhyme with the sounds of your soul.

☼ You always have power. Your problem is not knowing how to use it or not wanting to use it!

☼ Use your power, you silly two-legger. Imagine. Create. Be free!

☼ Wear your magic hat!

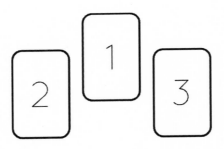

The Magic Hat

1. What is your greatest source of power and talent – something that is unique to you?

2. What power is needed right now to create the reality that you want?

3. How can you best channel and make use of that power?

High Priestess

For centuries, people and pandas alike come before the High Priestess. They seek an answer from her, hoping to gain truth and clarity from a wave of her paws, but to their surprise and sometimes dismay, she mostly only has questions. An abundance of them, in fact. Now that you are here, she casts you a curious look. Does she have the answer that you seek? Or do you?

The High Priestess resides in the Iridescent Forest, where semi-translucent plants glimmer blue and purple at night underneath the pale silver moon. She saunters around the forest, light as a feather and floating like a mystery. Nobody knows what she's thinking, but everyone knows that she's wise, and everyone wants her to answer their burning questions. When she tilts her head sideways, her beautiful headgear catching the moonlight and sparkling from her movements, she will smile her pretty panda smile. There seems to be a spec of light in her eyes, but you're not entirely sure. Why are you here again? Why have you found yourself in her woods? What do you truly seek?

Panda Power Up

The High Priestess looks up towards the sky, sighing to the moon and leaving you frustrated with your questioning. You continue to hurl your confusion at her, hoping that one of the questions will finally capture her attention. And perhaps, she will finally answer. She raises a paw to stop your fervent questioning, and she gestures you to sit beside her. Like the two pandas you previously met, she has a gift for you. She gracefully unlaces her celestial headgear, her Lunar Circlet – a series of sparkly trinkets on a strand of silver. She hands it to you gently. Now, this does not grant you the answers that you seek. It does help you ask the right questions, however.

HIGH PRIESTESS' GUIDE
TO CONQUERING THE WORLD

☼ You are the one to solve the riddles in your heart.

☼ Some answers are only seen in certain light.

☼ Some answers take their time as they make their way to you. Choose to meet them halfway, but never seek to hurry them. Otherwise, they get temperamental and may choose to lose themselves to unexpected detours as they wander off the road.

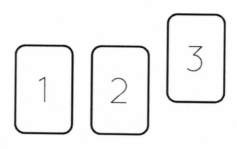

The Lunar Circlet

1. How can you create a relaxing and welcoming atmosphere so the answers that you seek will be glad to travel to you?

2. How can you tap into the space of waiting and the space of mystery within you? How can you expand your inner vision so that light may reveal the insight that you need?

3. What is the wisdom that is emerging within you? What is the answer that you will find and unearth?

The Empress

*The way she clasps her paws together and meets
your gaze with tenderness and admiration – you
would think that The Empress has spotted some
rare and precious treasure. She has indeed
discovered a wonderful treasure beyond measure –
she's found you.*

Wherever the Empress goes, spring follows. Seeds poke their
tiny heads out from the wet soil at the sound of her paw steps.
Grass spring into an ocean of green, and flowers flourish into
gardens – a soft colorful cosmos. She is a panda of gentle quiet
beauty, and there is music in the way she gracefully saunters.
Her children always come to her to borrow her staff, a shiny
rosy jewel and an emblem of her status. She lends it without
hesitation, for she knows her cubs will always return to her.
They are her real jewels – not the staff, nor her floral crown.
They are the real treasures – treasures that do not belong to her
but will always be beheld and cherished by her. She is the

Empress, and it is her divine destiny to give, to nurture, and to love without reserve.

Panda Power Up

Inevitably, you are drawn towards her – likes bumblebees to flowers and a homecoming tide towards sandy shores. The Empress would have let you borrow her magical pink staff and allow you to have a go of plant-bending, if only one of her cubs didn't take off with it earlier that day, that is. Humans seem to enjoy watching random vines and fruits spurt out from wherever they point, she says. But she promises you the next best thing. She reaches for you with both of her paws and draws you into a bear hug. She holds you close, and you feel tiny movements within your chest, against your ribcage. Your heart is expanding. Your soul is singing. Whoever you are, the dreams inside of you that are seeds – they are growing. They are flourishing. And they are becoming. The Empress has given you the bear hug of life.

THE EMPRESS' GUIDE
TO CONQUERING THE WORLD

☼ The Empress has loved you since the moment you are born, and into the future forever more.

☼ You are lovely, beautiful, and perfect in every way - you are a rare treasure, a precious gem to behold.

☼ A heart, a dream, a wish, a soul – let go of your hold of them, for they need space to grow.

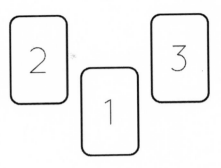

The Empress' Pink Staff

1. What stirs in your heart-space right now? What do you seek to nurture and grow? Is it you? Is it your dream and aspirations? You hold the Empress' pink staff (the panda cubs have returned with it and she's giving you a turn)

2. Witness it as it is: its beauty, its voice, its becoming. What do you see? What has it always been, what is it now and what will it become?

3. How can you hold space and channel power from a place of love – to nurture it, to give to it, to allow it to grow?

The Emperor

With a single wave of his paw, the Emperor gestures you to go to him, pointing at you with his regal staff – a wand made of deep encompassing gold and a lustrous gem of ruby. He seems unperturbed, radiating confidence and calm. Without blinking, he scratches his butt casually, wiggling his right leg and easing into the motion.

The Emperor sits, his aura sturdy and grounding, like the way the spine of a mountain range grips the earth and grapples the distant horizon – pulling the sky downwards like a hefty curtain. He does not accept bows, nor does he deem complicated salutations necessary. But if you insist on paying your respects, he will always bow back - being the courteous and respecting panda that he is. Then he will stand in his full height, reminding you of a panda's natural size, a size that is often forgotten or overlooked but inherent with strength and prowess. As he towers over you, he will pretend to hold the tension. Then he'll promptly break it in order to give you a genial bear hug – picking you up and squeezing you tightly in his arms with an uproarious, hearty laugh. That is his ritual – he is a panda king with a sense of humor, and he likes to make a point of it. There is nothing worst and more damaging than taking a bear's position of power too seriously.

Panda Power Up

You and the Emperor's eyes meet. Under the blazing sun, the gravity of his presence anchors you, calms you, and secures you. The panda king once again gestures at you with his staff, the majesty of his crown framing his chubby cheeks in a glorious fashion. Without hesitation, he dubs each of your shoulders with his wand, and you feel the heat of the ruby orb next to your cheeks. There is no need for words. The Emperor has proclaimed you his equal. A grandiose knightly episode is one of his favourite things to administer, and most of the time he merely does it for the fun of it. To him, he is merely pointing out the obvious: you are worthy, just as you have always been – and you will always be worthy, today and forevermore, as you stand in your own power.

THE EMPEROR'S GUIDE TO CONQUERING THE WORLD

☼ A panda's power is not measured by the number of his tummy folds – unless you unfortunately find yourself under them.

☼ Power isn't a beating stick. Nor is it a whip.

☼ Commit to being you. Don't ever apologize for who you are.

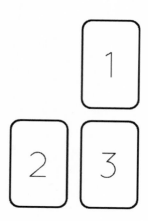

The Emperor's Ruby Staff

1. What's something shiny and fashionable that is making you look "powerful" right now? What is something you hope to acquire to accessorize yourself so you can look more powerful, more successful, ore authoritative?

2. How does that contrast the real power that you have within you? What is the real power within you – something that exists simply because you exist, something that cannot be taken away?

3. Where does real power come from?

The Hierophant

*He's the panda with the smug glasses, and he never
goes anywhere without his tie. The Hierophant
chews on a strand of bamboo grass, clicking his
tongue and giving you a cocky point of his chin.
"You're here to learn from me, I reckon," he begins.
"Straighten your pants, you filthy millennial."*

It is a truth universally known that the Hierophant's snout is
perpetually twitching in mild disapproval during a conversation.
He is old, but that shall not stop him from foaming puffs of
finely aged sass through his mouth and unto the world. He
makes a sport of wandering about the Panda Kingdom and
hunting down fresh curious minds – to give himself the chance
to showcase his uncanny ability to spawn a lecture about
anything, anybody and anywhere, with no prior planning or
consideration. Legend has it that he has once given a
spontaneous speech about the importance of patterning on a
single leaf that lasted about six and a half hours long – the
speech began from a green leaf's biological structure and its

properties and eventually progressed to the psychological effects of the various shades of green in art history, and eventually ended with the existential significance of sacred geometry within nature. Full of knowledge and chatty energy, he is a walking matrix of information and data that never fails to broadcast himself.

Panda Power Up

It is too late now – the Hierophant has spotted you and taken a keen interest in your disposition. Before you have the chance to escape, he places his furry paw on one of your shoulders to secure your audience. Without stopping to take a breath, he begins his lecture. Surprisingly, he tells you the history, cultural significance and archetypal memory that predate your existence – energies and forces and ancestral data that have come to affect you, the bigger pictures that you are inevitably part of. He easily names the prominent philosophers that may present a solution to your question, and he compares the different attitudes, mindsets, and customs of various peoples in your world that may give you insight into your conundrum.

You listen with full attention, only asking a few thoughtful questions when it is relevant. When the Hierophant is done, leaving you quite inspired and breathless, he gives you his crystal prism. "There are many things you can and *should* learn about the world," he says. "But don't take my word for it." Your eyes widen at such a remark. "I can teach you everything that I know, and I know a lot – mind you." He gives you a snobby wink. "Definitely more than you – that is certain. But you must decide for yourself where you stand in the multitude of ideas that will smother you alive if you are not careful with your thoughts. You must choose your thinking. That is the only way to learn." He says, and shoves the prism into your hands. "White light goes in, and a spectrum comes out. Remember everything that I've taught you, but find your own perspective. Honor your traditions, your cultures and your elders, but do not become burdened by it. Find your voice. And your light."

THE HIEROPHANT'S GUIDE
TO CONQUERING THE WORLD

☼ Knowledge is a source of learning and inspiration – allow it to empower you and your thinking.

☼ Choose your thoughts and your perspectives. Think for yourself.

☼ Traditions, cultures and customs are important to acknowledge, but they are not absolute.

☼ Know how you see the world and allow yourself to be seen.

☼ Straighten your pants.

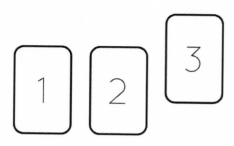

A Prism, Not a Prison, of Knowledge

1. What is something (a belief, a way of thinking or behaving) that you've been taught to think or do that has so far gone unquestioned?

2. How has it affected you and how is it relevant to the way you want to live your life right now?

3. How does this particular belief challenge, disrupt, amalgamate or add to your sense of identity and who you are as a person right now?

Lovers

As cherry blossom petals kiss and caress your cheek,
having glided towards you on the wings of a fresh
wind – you notice that two pandas have appeared.
They surround and sandwich you in the middle,
grabbing you by the hands. The fur on their paws
tickle your palm, and an inexplicable warmth
travels from your fingertips to the rest of your body.

Ah, the Lovers. Ever since that fateful evening where they found each other in an ocean of pink – the tall cherry blossom trees bend and dip their branches into an arch above them, celebrating their cosmic union – these two pandas have never been apart. They are each other's poetic opposites, forces that cannot be tamed, joined or reconciled except through mutual recognition, compassion and love. They will never be the same, but never will they ever seek to level each other's differences. They are the yin and the yang, the sky and earth. They have chosen to be together, each panda complete on their own yet made whole by each other's presence. Together, they are an experience, a continuum, an awareness, a moment to be had. Together, they are each other's world entire.

Panda Power Up

The Lovers guide you to the cherry blossom forest – the place where they saw and found each other. Barefoot, the dry leaves rustle and tickle your toes. There is a flurry in your heart – you feel a deep yearning as the sound of footsteps approach. A figure emerges from behind the cherry blossom tree, and as they come closer, you blink as you are suspended in disbelief. It isn't possible, because you were not expecting to see this person. It simply cannot be.

Yet you have always known this person – known them your whole life. You've fought with them, judged them, wept over them, and sought after their love. You've gone through thick and thin with them, and shared with them your woes and your triumphs. You wanted them to be everything, and at the same time they were never enough. As you steady your breath, you see the figure that bears resemblance to yourself stand before you. Is this really how you look? Naked and imperfect, yet every part of you familiar. The two of you near each other, and at the same time, you reach towards each other and find each other's hand. The pandas nod to each other, and as you bear witness to yourself and the harmony of your parts, they open their paper umbrella – and cast it over you to protect and bless your union.

THE LOVERS' GUIDE
TO CONQUERING THE WORLD

☼ In the storm that is your soul, the rain rages on – and you, a tiny boast lost at sea, searches and finds your shore.

☼ You are a beautiful paradox, never to be reconciled, but always to be loved.

☼ To be whole is to be complete within oneself.

☼ When the sun shines, we can shine together. Told you I'll be here forever. Said I'll always be your friend – took an oath that I will stick it out till the end.

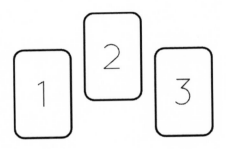

Under My Umbrella

1. What are two properties within your being that are constantly at odds with each other?

2. How do they push and pull against each other?

3. How do they make you unique and whole and complete?

The Chariot

The pandas are cheering as Victor's winged bike, Rainbowburst, makes a difficult S-shaped twirl in the sky, curling the cotton-candy clouds. The roar of the engine sends a jitter down your soul. You realize that there is nothing that is stopping you from doing what you've always wanted. Absolutely nothing.

When Victor needs to get somewhere, he first puts on his aviator hat for protection against high winds – a panda's gotta keep his head warm when he's flying! Then, with suave and the kind of confidence that only a biker-panda-dude can have, he hops on his winged motorbike (his bae), *Rainbowburst,* and takes it for a majestic ride. There's no need to stop at a gas station - for this magical vehicle is fueled not by gas, but by a panda's purpose. Every time Victor chooses to align his trajectory with his ultimate ambition and vision of success, Rainbowburst's engine revs and roars into life. Indeed, pandas aren't born to fly (and they most definitely do not wish to run), but nothing is stopping them from reaching and conquering the sky.

Panda Power Up

Before you realize, Victor has hurled himself at you and tackled you to the ground. He gives you a brotherly noogie and tells you that he'll be happy to take you for a ride. "Anywhere you want," he says. "Seriously, anywhere. Name it. Paris, the Himalayas, the edge of the Milky Way, or your wildest dreams. And we shall be there in a furry jiffy!" Rainbowburst's iridescent wings flutter in excitement, spitting out powerful colors as the two of you discuss your grand plans. Chariot is about success, and more importantly, succeeding in your own terms. Pandas aren't born to fly, but that, of course, doesn't stop or intimidate our bold visionary, Victor the Chariot Panda. He's found his own way of thriving and reaching for the sky. Let nobody define your limits or how you ought to succeed and thrive in life. Do it your own way. And mean it when you do it.

VICTOR'S GUIDE TO CONQUERING THE WORLD

☼ *Forward*, like a boss!

☼ If you can't fly, run. If you can't run, tumble. If you can't tumble, wiggle wiggle wiggle. Or, you know, find yourself a magical winged bike.

☼ Don't be afraid of getting lost. There's no such thing! Keep your engine running and just keep going!

☼ Reach for the stars – destiny awaits!

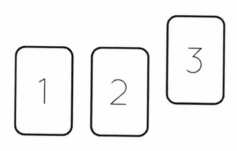

Rainbowburst

1. What revs your engine and makes your wings flutter and ready to take flight?

2. What destination unknown, or ultimate treasure that you are riding towards?

3. How can you ride that momentum to infinite success and beyond?

Strength

The dark creature shapeshifts in the shadows – it appears to be long, sinewy and serpentine for one moment, and bulky, monstrous and growling the next. Rapidly, it advances, and a brave little mouse flicks his nose and unsheathes his sword. Behind him, a panda sashays into view while gnawing a bamboo shoot.

Mousey Valentine is an expert swordsman – he's traveled far and wide across the animal spirit realm, searching for an opponent worthy of his skills. Stubborn and singularly proud, he did not expect to find his match in the Panda Kingdom, for pandas are not known for their readiness in combat. Yet, on a momentous occasion where he struggled to defeat a terrifying creature from the shadowlands, he met Hercules, who wasn't particularly strong in muscles, but was steadfast and unflurried in his stride. He came to Valentine's rescue – and Mousey watched incredulously as the shadow creature retreated and withdrew its malicious advances. "What did you do to prove to the monster that you were stronger?" he beseeched. "Tell me the secrets to your strength!" Hercules munched on his bamboo shoots and shrugged. "You want some bamboo?"

Panda Power Up

Mousey Valentine is often underestimated for his size, but he doesn't mind! He is a tiny warrior with a thirst for justice and the skills to win in any fencing duel. He offers you his sword and his service – should you need his talents in overcoming evil titans or summoning your own unique strength. On the other paw, Hercules is a common panda with the name of a mythic hero, who doesn't claim to be a warrior but does take pride in his enormous digestive capacity. He offers you the bottomless void that is his insides to help you stomach any negativity and woes in life. The world is so big, but his belly is even bigger. There is absolutely nothing that cannot be tackled and deconstructed by his fierce panda enzymes. With the help of Mousey Valentine and Panda Hercules, let nothing diminish you and chip away your strength!

A MOUSE AND A PANDA'S GUIDE TO CONQUERING THE WORLD

- ☼ Strength comes in all shapes and sizes
- ☼ Strength exists as an inner knowing.
- ☼ How other people choose to see you and shape you in their minds is none of your business.
- ☼ You are soft but unbreakable. Free and unshakable. Fluffy but savage. Cute but fierce.
- ☼ Stand tall as the hero your own brave tales.

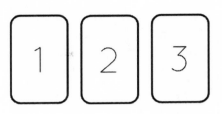

Cute but Fierce, Fluffy but Savage

1. What is something that challenges you and gives you a hard time? What seeks to diminish your strength?

2. What is your unique source of strength that gives you the mark of a hero and sets you apart?

3. How can you best unleash your power and channel the spirit of Mousey Valentine and Panda Hercules?

Hermit

Strange vivid colors shine bright and deep and
true – a panda takes his lamp into bamboos of blue.
There is ancient wisdom hidden within the
mushroom forest, and the hermit has heard its call.
The other pandas watch him as he turns and
vanishes into the depths of the glowing woods,
knowing that he disappears only to appear again,
and that he leaves only to return.

The fireflies in Solomon's lamp shimmer and cast a dim light –
the damp air and moth dust drifts and plasters themselves onto
the Hermit's nose. As night falls, the forest comes to life, aglow
with bright fantastical lights like the mysterious creatures of the
deep sea. Dragonflies weave in and out of neon mushroom
shrubs, and phosphorescent snails with their opal shells can be
seen crawling up blue stalks of bamboo. The Hermit finds his
secret cave. He enters it – the comfortable darkness wrapping
itself around him like a childhood blanket. Here, away from the
noises of the world, he is free to pursue his thoughts completely
unhindered. Alone but not lonely, he embarks on a journey to
reach the centre of his innerscapes, unraveling truth and
wisdom that are much needed for his growth.

Panda Power Up

The Hermit doesn't do this very often – but seeing that you are an invaluable friend to the panda-folk – he's decided to entrust you the exact location and coordinates of his secret hideout should you choose to embark on a journey into the Mushroom Forest. This strange eldritch place has a will of its own – its soul is labyrinthine and ancient, and it tends to have its own swirling space-time. It's very easy to get lost in there, but you shall not worry about that. The Hermit has placed an empty lamp by the edge of the mushroom forest and informed the fireflies that they are to treat you as their panda-kin. You will always have a light source, and the path towards wisdom shall never be closed or dim to you.

SOLOMON'S GUIDE
TO CONQUERING THE WORLD

☼ A panda needs his space to think.

☼ Always take the time to journey into your thoughts, but do not forget to return. Life awaits.

☼ Wanderers, seekers and wayfarers. Sometimes they lose their way to find their way again.

☼ Befriend the fireflies. They light up the road.

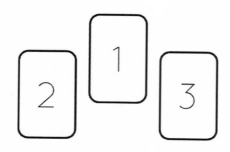

The Mushroom Forest

1. What does it feel like to enter your personal introspective space, away from the world? What does your "mushroom forest" look like and feel like?

2. How do you know when you need to retreat into your Hermit's Cave? What are the signs?

3. The fireflies know the way – they grow brighter when you get closer to your truths. How will you know when the truth that you seek is within your reach?

Wheel of Fortune

At the seaside fair, a band of pandas sounds their trumpets and drums in triple-time, a cheerful whimsical march. The wind brings you the scent of cotton candy, sweet dreams of blueberry and vanilla. From where you stand, you can see the Ferris wheel turn and rotate slowly to the beat of the music, while pandas in striped suspender shorts and baseball caps run around with bamboo-churros in hand.

Every morning, after a sizable bowl of bamboo oatmeal (absolutely soul-nourishing, mm!) Philip brushes and combs his fur and tumbles down to the Fair of Marvels by the seaside of Panda Kingdom. The ferret at the lollipop stand spots him from far away and immediately sets himself to work, dipping the butterscotch candy disc base into melted rainbow sugar. As soon as Philip arrives, the ferret holds up the lollipop to dry, airing it with a white paper fan. "Would ya look at 'tat, Mr. Panda," the ferret says with a ferret accent. "Five colors! And perfectly placed in stripes." Philip gives him a thumbs up. Every day, he never knows which pattern or color palette will greet him on his lollipop. Sometimes it's pumpkin orange with cream polka dots, and sometimes it's a delightful blend of pastel pink and baby blue. The ferret will always apologize when the dreaded emerald green with grey specs comes up, for he knows that particular combination of colors reminds the panda of moldy bamboo. When that happens, Philip will always grumble under his breath about his ill fortunes – *grah! Just my luck!* But at the end of the day, this panda doesn't seem to mind. The lollipop, no matter the color, tastes just as sweet – and as he walks towards his favourite attraction – the Ferris wheel – he knows the view on top will never fail to excite his heart.

Panda Power Up

Philip is a simple panda who enjoys simple pleasures. For this, he offers you a free voucher at the ferret's lollipop stand. It's for the rainbow dip sucker, the kiosk special. You never know what colors you will get on the lollipop – in fact, it may well be a color that you dislike, and that one yucky flavor may just end up coating your treat. Don't complain - the ferret has no control over the rainbow dip – it's a mysterious swirl of sugar that does whatever it pleases for the customers. No matter – it's okay if you find it distasteful. The ferret's lollipop is unpredictable like that – just like life. And who knows – you may get lucky next time and end up with something you've always wanted. No matter what kind of lollipop you get, you've got a friend in Philip. He's always down for the Ferris wheel ride with you.

PHILIP'S GUIDE
TO CONQUERING THE WORLD

☼ The Wheel goes up, and then it comes down. And then it goes back up again. Whatever happens – just enjoy the ride!

☼ Life is sweet. Just like a lollipop.

☼ You're never alone on this ride.

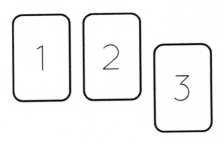

The Ferries Wheel of Life

1. Tickets, please! Just kidding. You are always welcome for the Ferris Wheel of Life. You're always on it, in fact. With that in mind, how would you like to experience your life today?

2. The wheel is spinning. How do you feel so far about this ride that you're on?

3. Don't look at me – I'm just a panda named Philip. I don't know how to make it better. How would you make it better? Another lollipop, perhaps?

Justice

The leg twitches, and with a meticulous maneuver of muscle – gentle but firm – the foot is in the face. The shadows stop promptly in their tracks, bouncing and rolling off the invisible barrier. The sword, shining in pristine silver, separates the light from the dark.

At the outskirts of the Panda Kingdom, Liam exercises frequently, keeping up with his squats and lunges. When he's finished with his workout, he settles down on the baby grass by his favourite patch of flowers, freshly sprung from the land he has reclaimed and is now protecting. Far away from his panda tribe, he dutifully tends to his tasks as one of the guardians of his world. Every day, gloomy clouds congregate at the borders and attempt to enter without the permission of the pandas. These dark energies will do anything to get in – sometimes they take the shape of your kin, appealing to your love and demanding your attention and compassion. Sometimes they manifest as hideous monsters, hissing and growling to inspire fear and submission. Those insidious things will do anything to lower your guard – and that is why the Panda Kingdom needs Liam. This panda is impartial to games and illusions and impossible to guilt-trip or frighten. With his sword in hand and his foot in place, he keeps the darkness at bay, It is arduous work, but Liam knows that it must be done. And so it shall be.

Panda Power Up

"This is how you lift your foot – look," Liam pulls his thigh up in the air and flexes his toes nimbly, as if to shoo unwanted critters away. "Make sure it's parallel and indicative of your boundaries," he says. "And push." He continues to walk you through the instructions – how to assert justice 101. How to say no. How to withdraw your consent and permission to things and people that no longer serve you and are taking up your personal space at your expense. You lift and you flex your foot a couple of times as Liam continues to correct your posture and angling. Before long, he is nodding in approval. "Good," he says. "This is how it's done. Now you are the proper guardian of your space." You gesture for his sword longingly, hoping to leave with something sharp to defend yourself with. Liam politely refuses. "I need this to balance the light in Panda Kingdom; it is my duty." He gives you a reassuring and comforting pat on your shoulder. "Besides, you don't need a sword. You're a sharp one! Just don't lose your edge."

LIAM'S GUIDE
TO CONQUERING THE WORLD

☼ Boundaries. They are important.

☼ Thank you, next.

☼ Keep negativity and shenanigans at bay by not allowing them in your life. Protect your space. Nothing enters your panda zone without your explicit permission.

☼ Say no – so you can say yes!

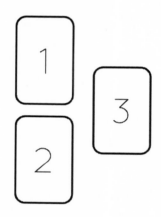

The Panda Foot

1. What is challenging your boundaries right now? What are you allowing, consciously or unconsciously, into your space?

2. Sorry, you're not coming in here. Remember the lessons Liam has taught you. Use the leg move. What can you do to maintain your boundaries in a way that protects yourself but does not harm others?

3. You're sharp as a sword! What is your truth and how can you stand behind it?

The Hanged Panda

The fireflies gather around the hanging panda, whose arms are shaking from the strain. This is terrible, he thinks, and he can't seem to remember how he's gotten himself in this embarrassing situation – yet he does not dare to move. The feather. The feather on his nose. Anytime now. Anytime.

Hank saw this happen differently in his imagination when he climbed the tree enthusiastically, hoping the catch the mysterious feather from the sky. It was glowing, and a song seemed to be drifting with it as it landed on his nose. Now, he's a few tickles away from an epic sneeze, and he's definitely regretting cutting back on his core training at his local pilates class. The instructor was right – your core really does carry the rest of your body. With his strength dwindling by the second, he is unsure how long he can keep hanging on. He desperately wishes to move and adjust his position, but he's afraid to lose the feather. *Just a little longer,* the fireflies seem to encourage him. *Just a little longer.*

Panda Power Up

Ha! Of course. It's just occurred to Hank that his mission is to catch the feather – and it really doesn't matter *how* or *where* he catches it. How silly of him – the answer has been there all this time – right under his nose! He sneezes and the feather takes off into the air, swirling and dancing and beginning to fall. Hank lets go of one of his hands to allow the rest of his body to fall through the branches of the tree. Swiftly, he hugs the tree trunk and lowers himself to the ground – grip after grip. The feather falls right into his hand – perfect timing – just as he opens his paw to receive it. He gives you a triumphant look and playfully jiggles his belly fat – taking pride in his one pack ab. He gives you a thumbs up. "Don't give up," he says. "Nobody is ever truly stuck in life!"

HANK'S GUIDE
TO CONQUERING THE WORLD

☼ You skip core work, your core skips you when you need it to work. So don't skip your core work. Hank recommends pilates.

☼ Keep calm and panda on – even if it's awkward!

☼ Just because you can't see something right away doesn't mean you will never see it.

☼ A lot of problems tend to solve themselves – no need to try so hard.

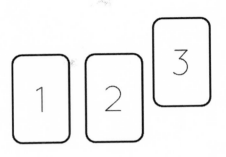

Panda Sit-Ups

1. What is your current predicament? What's something that you're fixated on – something that's jamming your system? What's "keeping you hanging"?

2. What is the strength, awareness or wisdom that you need to cultivate right now so you can pull a ninja double-jump and flip your problem on its head?

3. What will set you free from this awkwaaaaaard situation so you can keep calm and panda on?

Death

*In the end, there is silence. A panda closes his eyes
forever, moss creeping into his fur. She sits, her
heart beating against her ribcage – each thump as
loud and unbearable as the next.*

Life is death, and death is life. That is the truth. That is the very
nature of existence. The Panda Kingdom is never absent of life,
for in the presence of death, life quietly returns. Life is
everywhere, and so is death. Death is the rhythm of the
Universe – the ringing space between each cosmic breath.
Pandas know this, though this knowledge never really eases
their pain. During such moments, they remind themselves to
breathe. They do not bury their grief – instead, they plant a
flower there, a flower that will encase the flesh and bones of
what they have lost. As they watch the flower blossom, they let
life begin again.

Panda Power Up

A single, orange flower sits before you, nodding and wobbling from the droplets of rain. The sky is brightening, and light is peaking through the clouds. You hear a panda nearby, paws on wet ground, one after another, approaching you. She lowers her head to sniff the flower, and looks up at you to meet your eyes. You feel a wave of serenity wash over you, clearing away the grime, the ash and the debris that you've been carrying in your soul, weighing you down. Without knowing how, or why, you see the life of the orange flower unfold in your mind – you see the little seedling finding its home in this soil, you see the stem crawl out of the earth like a little hand doing a morning stretch, and you see it green and grow into the beauty that it is now. You can't explain it, but you feel different. The world that you know is no longer the same. It has shifted ever so slightly and imperceptibly – and yet, as you look back over your shoulder, you see that you are now lightyears away, a universe apart from where you once stood.

DEATH'S GUIDE
TO CONQUERING THE WORLD

☼ Everything changes, and nothing stays the same.

☼ Flowers bloom and blossom at your feet with each step that you take.

☼ Flowers crumble into dust and return to ash at your feet with each step that you take.

☼ Breathe. Remember to breathe.

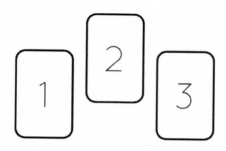

A Single Flower

1. What is ending? What is the part of you that is dying?

2. Why are you fighting it? What is stopping you from accepting the truth?

3. What is the flower that shall blossom – the life that shall bloom after this death?

Temperance

*The panda clasps her paws and closes her eyes to
the sound of flowing water rushing through hollow
bamboo, the currents ebbing towards the edge of the
pool, caressing the cool grey stones. The birds chirp
and chime in their riddles and sing-songs, echoing
in the distance.*

When Mellon is sitting in the Garden, unmoving, the pandas
will usually tiptoe around her to avoid disturbing her. They
think that she is in deep contemplation and meditation –
perhaps she is traveling across galaxies and nebulas towards the
cosmic wild unknown with her mind. That cannot be further
from the truth, however. She is present, and she is merely
listening - very much aware of her surroundings. To be honest,
Mellon doesn't really mind if others "interrupt" her, for there is
nothing to interrupt. There is only the Moment, and the
Moment after. Each Moment is Now just as it is Forever. There
is no other Moment other than the one we're in now – the
time-space and space-time where our intention flows.

Panda Power Up

Mellon welcomes you into her Garden of Temperance. There is no judgment here. No worry. No measurement. No ticking of the clock. It is a space where you enter to be relieved of time, for there is only a single moment – the moment that you embody right now. The moment that you breathe in, and then the moment where you breathe out. In, and out, and repeat. If you're unable to flow into the Moment, enter the Garden of Temperance and sit next to Mellon – her rhythmic breathing and steady heartbeat will calm you. She's also available for therapeutic hugs if you're craving some. Between you and me – being the chubbiest panda in the Panda Kingdom, Mellon is the best panda to hug and cuddle with. Just don't fall asleep under her.

MELLON'S GUIDE
TO CONQUERING THE WORLD

☼ "The past is history, and tomorrow is a mystery. Today is a gift, and that is why it is called the present." - a very wise turtle once said.

☼ A panda is black and white, but a panda is a panda - nothing more, and nothing less.

☼ Not too loose and not too tight - right in the middle, the feeling is just right.

☼ Breathe. You are a breath of life.

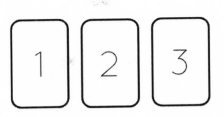

A Panda Moment

1. What is currently glitching your system and distracting you from your sense of alignment and ease?

2. How can you enter the space of Temperance, the space of Now and ultimate panda peace?

3. How can you stay in its awareness, and carry the spirit of Temperance wherever you go?

The Devil

"I trusted you."

The iron collar tightens around the panda's neck, the spikes dig into its fur and tearing at its neck as it struggles against the metal links. You stand there numbly, listening to its whimpers, watching it suffer deeply – watching its tears fall. Who would do such a thing? Who would hurt a creature so innocent, and so precious? Who could put a cold collar around the neck of a panda, to take away its freedom? You wonder if there's anything you can do to set it free. You approach it as it lets out a desperate cry and shrinks from you. It won't let you get close, but you are determined to undo this injustice. You pick up the heavy chains tied to its neck, and link by link you trace it to its source, hoping to find a hook, a lock, or something to unfasten to return the panda to its freedom. As you come upon the last few links, you recoil from shock and horror as you discover its source. The link – the metal link. The chains. The other end of the chain. It is firmly clasped around your wrist – with blood dripping down from your own hand.

Panda Power Up

Ah, now you remember. You remember what you did to betray something so pure. How could you? What did you hope to gain in exchange? What did you hope to forget – to bypass? What did you think was going to happen when you sacrificed and betrayed your inner panda? Your inner self? The part of you that is as pure and precious as a panda? Did you really feel more powerful? More content? More at peace? The profit, the fame, the glory, the pseudo-joy that you managed to acquire at the expense of your personal truths, your integrity, and your boundaries – at the suffering of your inner panda – however you justify it – is a betrayal to yourself and no one else. *You* did this. You caused it to suffer. Don't blame it on the devil, and don't blame it on anyone else. As you hurt your inner panda, you are ultimately hurting yourself. Now that you've seen the chains and the blood on your hands – now that you've seen the wounds you have caused, to others and to yourself, with or without meaning to – you must take responsibility for what you have done. This is the only way to break apart from the devil's grasp – your own grasp. This is the only way to heal, and to be free.

LISTEN.

☼ The best way to transcend your pain and your limitations is to face them.

☼ Your inner panda trusts and loves you unconditionally, despite the pain and suffering you may have put it through.

☼ Only you have the power to set yourself free.

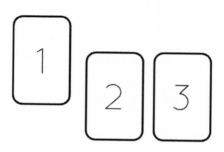

A Message from Your Inner Panda, Your Most Precious Self

1. This is what you're really doing to your inner panda – your innermost self, your spirit.

2. Why are you doing this?

3. How can you stop? Why do you need to stop?

The Tower

In his paw, a bolt of lightning.

Poison. There was poison in the stalk, and it was seeping into the soil like a growing disease, smothering and slowly killing its neighbours. *Goodbye, my friend.* It was decided, and though it pained him to say so, Zeus knew it must be done. So he fastened his gauntlet, curled his paw into a fist. As pure panda power surged through him, an electrifying storm raged in his chest and traveled to the rest of his body. He faced the bamboo tree and its sickening structure with determination, and in his paw, a bolt of lightning. *I am ready. I am ready now.* First, there was zap – a roar, a thunderous clap of a god. Then the sound of bamboo coming undone, shattering into a thousand splinters – broken bits and pieces tearing and shredding the heavens apart. From the fresh wound, a looming and breathing vacuum, lost hearts darted frantically about like frightened kites in the sky – caught in the whirling chaos of cacophony and destruction.

Panda Power Up

What ensued the destruction of the bamboo – the Tower moment, as humans like to call it – was this. Zeus wept. His heart shattered with the bamboo he had just destroyed – it had been a labour of his love. He knew it as a seed and watched it grow. But it couldn't have been helped. It must be done, as it was for the greater good. A Tower moment is never easy. Knowing this and thinking this, he looks to your direction. He unfastens his gauntlet, and he beckons you to wear it. This is his gift to you. *Do not be afraid*, he says. *You are ready – you always have been. New life is seeking to come through you. Do not fight it; your war is not with yourself. Let it course through you and fill you with its power. You are a crisscrossing blade of light, searing through the mythical darkness, destroying all that you weren't – so that you can be all that you are.*

ZEUS' GUIDE
TO CONQUERING THE WORLD

☼ You are the lighting and the thunder. A kung fu panda capable of striking down walls, barriers, mazes and prison bars.

☼ Search and destroy.

☼ Courage, dear heart.

☼ May the Force be with you.

☼ Don't step on a lego.

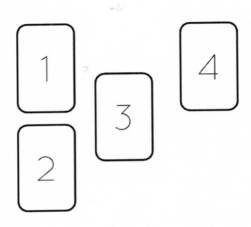

In Your Hand, a Bolt of Lightning

1. Smash through those bricks. What is no longer serving you and what structures are in need of some "constructive" destruction right now?

2. In your hand, a bolt of lightning. What is the best time to deliver the ultimate strike? What do you need to do to channel Zeus' power?

3. Thundering pain. Yes, it hurts. It's almost always a painful thing. What is breaking, disintegrating and collapsing right now? How does it make you feel?

4. Lightning courses through your veins, and power awakens from within. How can you best make use of this incredible power to bend and structure reality to your will, for your highest good, and the highest good of all?

The Star

Humming a tune to herself, Celia gazes upon the stars that blanket the sky in a sparkly haze – little gems that shine and glisten across the night's canvas, twinkling to the rhythm of her heart.

Every night, at the hour when the yellow star shines the brightest – you will find Celia sitting on the celestial branch, gazing into the wondrous flowing painting above. This is her secret corner – high above the ground, a cozy, magical dwelling only she has access to. Once she settles into a comfortable position, she will set her bowl aside, gently tipping it over and allowing the muddy water to flow out of the container. As the water cascades down from the branch, Celia will sing and whisper to it slowly. No, they are not being disposed of. They are being set free. *It's okay now; there's nothing to fear. You are safe. You are free from ghosts and goblins and monsters that plague you. you are safe. The stars are watching over you. They will protect you. And tomorrow will be a better day.*

"Only in the darkness can you see stars – and only in silence will you hear their songs and voices."

Panda Power Up

Celia invites you to sit with her on the celestial branch. She gestures with her paws for you to pick your favourite spot. You shift uncomfortably, fearing that the branch will fail to support your weight. As you tiptoe awkwardly, your hands outstretched for balance, you are surprised to find that the tree is sturdy and has not even wobbled once. You sit down next to Celia, her healing furs lightly rustled by the high winds. The bowl, though no longer supported, is now emptying itself. *There is something in the water – something familiar.*

You watch as the contents leave the bowl and disappear into the heights below, and bit by bit, you feel a change in you. A welcoming change. Celia gives you a happy nod. "You figured it out!" she gives you a thumbs-up. You nod back and reply, "Yes." Indeed, you *have* figured it out. As you let go of your past and bid it goodbye – as you allow your regrets, your pain and your sorrows to pour out of the bowl that is your heart – you become lighter. Your heart no longer feels heavy, your spirit as light as a butterfly wing. There are a breeze and a spaciousness in you and all at once, you feel safe. You feel safe from your difficulties and your troubles. You feel serene, at ease, at peace, and untouched by your past.

CELIA'S GUIDE TO CONQUERING THE WORLD

☼ Don't lose hope. Tomorrow will be a better day!

☼ The stars will sing for you. Now and always.

☼ And your dreams are trying to reach you. Always and forever!

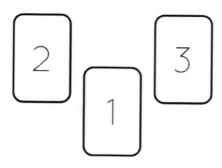

Starry Starry Night

1. What is weighing down your heart, your soul?

2. Reach for the stars. What is the wonder just beyond your reach – the dreams that are getting closer and closer to you as we speak? Even if you don't see it – they are there. Reach out to them. Connect with them. Beckon them to come to you, because they will.

3. How do your vision and hope rejuvenate you and heal you?

The Moon

Nonsense rhymes, mismatched socks. She's left her sleeping cap on, as the moon beneath her paws slowly rotates and turns on its axis, drifting up and down, in and out of orbit. Is this reality, or a very real dream?

Something's not right, Jellybean thinks to herself. If something isn't right, then something must be wrong – but she isn't quite certain. In fact, she isn't certain of anything right now. Is it still gravity that is anchoring her down, or is it the weight of her heart? Landscapes shift, and the clouds discolor the sky while glowing insects fly. She seems to be alone in the shadowscapes – where there are laughter and fairy wings in the mist, claws and teeth in the fog. Is this a dream, a nightmare, a fragmented and disjointed world drowning in her imagination? Where to, now? What do you do when there is no path to tread, no proper sight to behold, and nowhere to go?

Panda Power Up

Do not worry about Jellybean – this isn't her first time venturing into the depths of the panda lunarscapes. Being a panda with a loose sense of direction, she's prone to getting lost as she attempts the meandering paths of the Moon's strange, shifting world. As she journeys into the heart of this slumbering land where subtle things are alive beneath her feet – tiny bugs that she sees as cute one moment but swells and multiplies into something monstrous and utterly eerie within a single breath – she may seem lost, but indeed, she isn't. The trick is to remain curious. The moon path always finds its travelers when they are in dire need of clarity and direction – and if you find yourself drifting and traveling down the paths of lunarscapes, remember that there is something you are meant to find here, in the confusing and shifting darkness. And if you find yourself dwelling in this labyrinth for way too long and unable to find an exit – fear not - Jellybean to the rescue! While this dreamy panda can't always keep track of her noses, she has a talent for finding wayward humans with a confused and angsty look on their faces. She'll keep you company as the two of you journey to find the light.

JELLYBEAN'S GUIDE
TO CONQUERING THE WORLD

☼ Sometimes, the monsters in the dark are creatures bred from our own oppression and neglect.

☼ Strangely, your ghosts and your goblins always know where your light is hidden.

☼ Always wear a purple sleeping cap woven with premium bamboo cotton and panda blessings. It'll keep your head warm and stop you from losing your head altogether.

☼ You're the only one that knows your way home. Trust yourself to find it.

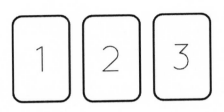

Pandas in Space

1. What is tugging at your conscious mind and in need of exploration right now?

2. What's lurking in the lunarscapes of your mind...what is secretly driving your desires, your fears, your impulses, and your choices?

3. What stories control you, and what can you do to release them and integrate them? So that they become part of your power, instead of holding power over you?

The Sun

Light on the horizon – a bright day melting away the night. The sun rises at the edge of the world, chasing away shadows and curses. The light you've been searching for – it's been inside you all along.

From afar, Yang Yang sees you as you emerge with Jellybean at the edge of the half-lit lunar world. The two of them are best friends and love each other dearly, but the only time they meet is when they part. Such is their way. The panda waves as Jellybean whirls herself around and disappears into the meandering paths of the moon world – no doubt getting her nose lost again, Yang Yang thought, bemused. She is a happy panda full of sunshine and light, and she lives in the open fields of Panda Kingdom, where the grass is green, the wind is free, and the hills are aliiiiiiiiiiiiiiive with the sound of muuuuuuuuusic. She rises with the morning (she *is* the morning) – and the world wakes when she wakes. She readies herself with a deep breath, the sunflower petals expand and blossom, stretching towards the sky as if to give it a hug. Then, beams and shockwaves of light radiate out of her being, setting the world bright and ablaze.

Panda Power Up

Yang Yang is glad to see you – her tail is twitching and vibrating with joy as you near. She volunteers to sit by you, shaking her sunflower petals back and forth like a proud mane – to shine upon you with her ultimate panda light – to bask you in truth, purity and freedom. You feel a tingle on your chin and the side of your cheeks, traveling down to the rest of your body. You feel like a solar being, a complete divine presence – how can you be just one person, so small and so infinite at the same time? You're jazzed with life and light. You're a sunflower basking in the glory of a morning. As Yang Yang gestures, fans, pokes and pretends to shoot fireballs out of her paws at you – all the while sharing her light and shining it towards your direction – you can't help but join her in her playful dance. The two of you, panda and human, hand in paw in hand, dancing in the sunlight with giant sunflower bibs, looking funny and liberated and forever free.

YANG YANG'S GUIDE TO CONQUERING THE WORLD

☼ Don't worry, your face won't turn into a sunflower waffle.

☼ Shine your light every single day. The world needs it. *You* need it, most of all.

☼ You're a miracle. A glowing jewel. A shining star.

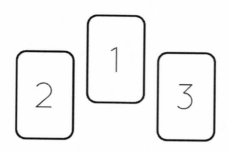

Sunny-Side Up

1. What is the truth that liberates you, allowing your joy and purity to shine forth?

2. What is the optimism that uplifts you, keeping your spirits high and radiant?

3. What is the trust that opens you up, grounding you in clarity and power?

Judgment

The blare of the trumpet reverberates through the air, the vibrations reaching Xavier in his sleep. With a start, he quickly sits up, fumbling in the grass as feathers and dragonflies take to the air in flight. And then he remembers.

Holy Bamboos! Xavier did not mean to fall asleep, but he is a very sleep-prone panda, indeed. It wasn't long before he felt the weight of his eyelids drew their heavy curtains close, and he curled into a ball to snuggle with himself on the lush grass of the Cosmic Garden. As he snored away, completely and utterly forgetting himself, he slowly forgot what it meant to be awake. Ah, the comfort of sleep. Naps under the luminous sun. The comfort of his snout resting in the fur of his arms. Ah, sleep. Except it was no time to be sleeping – the sun is shining in the sky, the grass is green and the wind is free! His fellow pandas were waiting for him to join them, and seeing no sign of Xavier, they took matters to their own paws. That was when the trumpet sounded and blasted Xavier in the face. Now that he's awake, he happily remembers what he's meant to be doing, and he joins his friends on the Garden of the Cosmos, singing and celebrating life – the joy of being alive.

Panda Power Up

Xavier is quite excited to get his hands on the trumpet that his panda friends used to wake up moments earlier. After learning of its properties and how it functions, this naughty panda is eager to test it out in the field. By "field" - he really means *you*. You best be on the lookout for a mischievous panda running towards you with a golden instrument in his paws – he is definitely up to no good and he's got a lot of lung power. If you've been sleepwalking and slumbering through the days, if you've been feeling disconnected and disassociated from your purpose and the meaning of life – you're just the "guinea pig" that Xavier needs to test out his new toy. He's prepared to give you a full blast, the full ringtone of the cosmic alarm clock with no snoozes – to have you so awake and shook that you won't be staggering through life like a barely conscious zombie anymore. Oh, don't worry, you'll definitely know it's him.

XAVIER'S GUIDE
TO CONQUERING THE WORLD

- ☼ Don't press snooze on the life you're meant to live!

- ☼ When you decide to wake up and finally get out of bed, the Universe and the pandas celebrate!

- ☼ It's okay if you snore. Xavier snores louder.

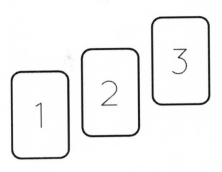

The "Song" of the Trumpet

1. Are you a zombie? What entraps you in your sleep? What is disconnecting you from the Universe, from the people around you, from yourself, from what you're meant to do and who you're meant to be?

2. Xavier blows pure trumpet into your ear. Loudly. Time to get up! You got work to do! Joy to cherish! Dreams to chase! A life to live! What is your panda wake-up call? What are the signs all around you?

3. Xavier pours a bucket of water onto your face. Cold water. With panda-shaped ice cubes (Xavier got the silicone molds on sale at Pamazon). What happens if you don't wake up now? What happens if you don't pay your dues, step up, start kicking butt, and start living life as you should?

The World

*As the earth slowly turns on its axis, locking itself
into place to finish a cycle – another rotation
swiftly begins. The crisp and airy sound of the
bamboo flute always signals the upcoming epilogue,
and the emergence of a prologue. Here you are, at
last.*

At the beginning of the galaxy, Nova was there to witness its
birth. She is ancient, older than the Hierophant – older than
any beings that are known to spirt kind. But her existence shall
not be measured by her years, for she is a panda transcending
both space and time. She is both young and old, forever and
impermanent at once. She ties a red ribbon to her bamboo flute
and plays, beckoning long lost wayfarers to come home. She's
been doing this forever, yet in a moment, the music will fade
and this too will pass. As the globe turns on its axis, Nova sees
the Fool and her Little Red Panda trot after her, leaping into the
great unknown. She sees all of pandakind, their charms, their
woes, their struggles and their endeavors. She sees the entire
timeline unfold, pieces and fragments and memories
crisscrossing into the buzzing matrix that is the never-ending

story – the narrative that continues to unfold. This is the end, but it is also the beginning.

Panda Power Up

Here you are, you have completed your quest – your quest of arriving, of becoming the person that you know yourself to be, the highest version of yourself that you can possibly be and more. It is the person that you have always been, the person who is like earth - always spinning, always moving, always growing, always turning on its axis, and always arriving back at where you started to begin again. Nova sees you for who you are. She plays the flute to celebrate your arrival – your return, and soon, your departure. Sooner or later you will always find yourself here: on top of the world, and the beginning of a new world. This is who you are. This is how things go. You will travel the world yet again – this time, with more wisdom, more resolve, more soul. And then you will arrive here, and you will see Nova again. And once more, she will play the flute for you, for the tales that you've lived and told, from the songs that you now sing.

NOVA'S GUIDE
TO CONQUERING THE WORLD

☼ Here you are, the entire world at your feet, in the palm of your hand.

☼ You only live once, but always you begin again.

☼ The end is only the beginning. Tell the Fool Nova says hi.

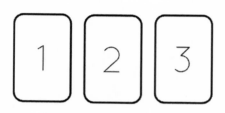

I Can Show You the World

1. I can show you the world. This card will represent who you are now, after you've come so far.

2. Shining, shimmering, splendid. This card will represent who you have always been – the highest version of yourself that you discover only to find that it's within you all this time.

3. The world is in your hands – now rock it! How can you best rock your world and shine forth your light as you complete your lessons and embark on a new journey?

The Minor Arcana

THE ELEMENTAL PANDAS: THEY ARE FIRE, AIR, WATER AND EARTH

The pandas from the elemental kingdoms each have their own stories to tell as well as wisdom to share. The Fire Pandas, the Air Pandas, the Water Pandas and the Earth Pandas are all full of eagerness and enthusiasm when it comes to helping humans and arbitrating our drama and first world problems (khem). Like the Majors, they are beyond excited to meet you and they are ready to receive and welcome you whenever you are ready. In fact, you best hurry to the Fire Pandas – they're getting feisty (and hungry) at your snail reading pace!

SUIT OF WANDS

The Fire Pandas

The Fire Pandas are ready for you whenever you are ready to embark on exciting new adventures, or when you need to flex your creative muscles to showcase your talents. They will cheer you on and help you smash through your fears with expert warrior moves and kung-fu bamboo staffs (to be promptly consumed as sustenance after a battle is fought and won).

Nothing dims a Fire Panda's playful energy, fighting spirit and thirst for life.

Life is a never-ending story – an everlasting adventure

Fire Pandas see life as a never-ending adventure and they are always looking for new ways to exercise their limbs and get some adrenaline pumping. Life is good. Life is wonderful. Life is pandatastic when these furry fireballs get to do whatever they want and whenever they want – and they are perfectly happy to "encourage" you to do the same. By "encourage", uh, I really mean that they will drag you by the hand, summersault all over you until they can get you away from your burdens and your woes, and wrestle you until you are laughing from your belly. Which is great, by the way. Fire Pandas are always down for a good laugh and a good fun session – what's the point of being alive if you're not enjoying yourself a little? What's the point of being a panda if you can't let your inner fire ignite into light? Do what you want to do. Laugh. Play. Be silly. Punch an imaginary enemy in the air with Accapella sound effects. *Come to life.*

Fearless and unstoppable: learn their Panda-Fu!

Fire Pandas know too well that they're "cuteness overload" – but that certainly doesn't stop them from being fierce and formidable! These unstoppable pandas never back down from a challenge, always choosing to face their fears and obstacles head-on. They are always ready to put up a good fight and show you some of their best moves! So if you are in need of some fearless panda-fu, summon the Fire Pandas to your cause. They are always happy to paw someone in the face for you. Or, if they don't get to do that, they are perfectly willing to stand by your side and be your cheerleading army. They will cheer so hard and clap so loudly that you can't help but feel good about yourself. They will channel all the fire they can muster into your soul, into your being so you will burst open with light and take flight!

YOU CAN CALL ON THE FIRE PANDAS FOR A FLAMING PAW BOOST IF YOU ARE:

☼ Seeking to unleash your creativity through an exciting new project or venture

☼ Planning to take a leap of faith to pursue your life's calling and your dreams

☼ Vigorously manifesting and mobilizing yourself through passionate action

☼ Needing to feel more confident, more self-assured, more awesome, more bomb!

☼ Needing a burst of insane courage to change lives, alter fates, and forge destiny!

☼ Getting ready to conquer fears, defeat your shadow enemies, and obtain ultimate panda victory!

PONDERING PANDA

☼ What makes you feel alive and unstoppable – as if an army of Fire Pandas are standing behind you and screaming your name?

☼ What makes you laugh? And not just laugh – belly laugh?

☼ In what ways are you courageous? What moves you and inspires you to rise to the challenge, to evolve, and to become bigger than your fears?

Activating Your Inner Fire Panda: A Ritual for Conquering Your Fears

Read and recite this passage for an instant Fire Panda Power Boost – for the moments when you are afraid and paralyzed with fear – the moments where you feel like you are undoubtedly going to fall – but you rise. You rise, instead.

It's there. It's right there. Look your fear in the eye. Flick your nose, Bruce Lee Style. When you're ready (which you are, always), you unleash your big move. The Fire Pandas are with you. They stand behind you and unleash fireball after fireball – shooting pure explosions of energy into your body, charging you with their light and their fire. Know this: you cannot be defeated. You have never been defeated and you never will. No, you are not bending your knee today!

You summon your courage, your resolve, your daring, your vitality, your passion – all that makes up who you are – and you move. You move swiftly, and you move fiercely. You are thunder and lightning in motion, a roar and a burst of laughter – a fire. You pull that fire from every inch of your being, and as that energy moves through you, you grab your fear by the throat, and you say,

You have no power over me. I am bigger than you. I am bigger and stronger than you will ever be. Today, I win. Just like I shall win again tomorrow. Day after day after day until forever.

Now you watch the life drains from the face of your enemy. And you know that your fear has no more power over you. Not now, not ever. You are the legendary Kung Fu Panda – a true warrior. And you know in your heart that you will always be stronger than your fear, and that your fears will never, ever win.

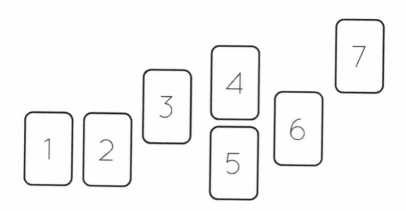

Kung Fu Panda Spread (Expanded)

When you need to do some serious butt-kicking and channel some epic heroism – use this spread to unlock maximum power and pawesomeness.

1. **Stretch Sesh.** What do I need to master in order to establish a solid foundation for channeling my power?

2. **Fighting Stance.** What do I need to do to get in the panda zone for some serious butt-kicking?

3. **HI-YAH!!** No mercy! This is how I'm going to rock and roll! How do I unleash maximum panda power to conquer any challenge that comes my way?

4. **The Monster Rears Its Head.** How is my fear trash-talking me right now, seeking to discourage me and strip me of my power?

5. **Hope is Frail.** Shadow clouds hover above – what does my fear show me? What is the outcome I am trying to avoid?

6. **The Hero Rises.** Yes, I am afraid, but I am also courageous. What is my strength, my courage, my resolve – that defines me as a hero of my own story, and the warrior that I am?

7. **The Ultimate Move!** It is time to show fear my true powers and finish it off with style! What is my big move? What makes me a champion?

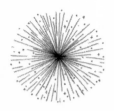

Ace of Wands

Your powers are yours to define, yours to shape, and yours to unleash. Only you can show the world your true colors – so explode with rivers of stars and rays of colors! You are infinite. You are brilliant. You are a star, a supernova, a galaxy spinning into light.

Ethan wears sunglasses (no – it's not Ray-Ban – if you're going offer a pair, however, this panda will accept it gladly) because each time he fires up his magic, an explosion of light-waves and fire-flares thunders and ripples outwards, pandafying all that crosses its path. Pandas aren't particularly showy when it comes to their power, but they definitely have that playful and giddy confidence – the kind where you know you're awesome and you kind of grin at yourself a little. If you stare at the card long enough, you may just hear a few "hehehe's" and "hyuk hyuk hyuks'". Now, come closer. Ethan is ready to shower you with a galactic blast of Panda Fire. "Time to conquer the Universe," he says. "And create whatever the bamboo you want in life! The earth will shake and tremble at your glory!"

WHAT FUELS YOU WITH POWER?

What lights your inner fire? What fills you with power and confidence and passion? What inspires you to grow, to dream big – and most importantly – what is calling out to you, beckoning you to take action? Go big – or go home!

IS SOMEONE TAIL-GATING YOUR BUTT WITH A HOT TORCH?

If you feel like someone is tail-gating your butt with a hot torch, close enough to burn your bushy tail – you either need to roll out of the way so you can put a stop to this hot reactionary mess that you are in – OR, you can always turn around, stomp your wand into the ground and affirm your fire with a burning declaration. Who's in control? You are. Who's the grand creator of your reality? You are. Don't let life or others trample over your desires. Live the life you want to live! Fire Pandas are rooting for you!

Seriously though – do you have a pair of Ray Ban? Ethan is collecting, and his birthday is coming up.

Two of Wands

What should I choose? Monsters lurk and roam; muscles tense and explode as legend and glory bubble to unfold. Two paths lay before me – two destinies unknown – what will I find, and where will I go?

Samuel's brain is fuzzy just thinking about where he should head next! Pandas generally have no trouble following their hearts (a.k.a. their stomach), and Samuel's stomach is churning and hungry for adventure! Dare he crosses the Shadow Bamboo Forest and faces the monsters in the dark – so that he could drink from the Sparkly Sparkling Lake with the hopes of gaining Eternal Cuteness? Or should he venture into the Valley of Willow Dragons, where the only danger is the lengthy, meandering stories that the old dragons like to "force" upon you before they allow you passage? Either way, this panda has massive plans to take over the world, and he's contemplating where he should start! There are new stages to unlock, and exciting new terrains to explore. As he eagerly decides where he should head next – he keeps his compass and his map nearby to craft the perfect plan for ultimate conquer. "The world is yours," he says. "You can go wherever you want to go! Except for the patch of bamboo by the Hermit's Cave. That patch's mine. Paws off!"

THE WORLD IS YOURS

Just like what Samuel said – the world is yours, and it is time for some epic expansion. What are some unknown areas on your map that you have yet to explore? Or are there places where you want to visit again, but this time, with more courage, more insight, and a better game-plan? Are there monsters or boss levels that you finally feel ready to take on?

DON'T FORGET TO CHECK YOUR COMPASS

If you're not sure where you want to go next or you feel burdened by your limiting beliefs and lethargy – do not worry. Samuel is an expert cheerleader and navigator – and he is here to motivate you and guide you! He is placing his fire paw on your shoulder right now to supercharge you with panda energy – so take a moment to absorb it! He is also lending you his special panda compass: almost always, this compass points to your Truth North, which is the direction of your coffee – I mean – your calling, your purpose, and your joy – so check in with it often.

Three of Wands

Can you see what's beyond these colors, just over there by the horizon? That's my heart. And my future. Yes, they are together already. They are united and they are one – I just need to get my butt over there.

Bree is feeling fuzzy and fizzy with optimism. Clusters of crystal and precious gems begin to grow all around her – synchronicities and good vibes swarming and mobilizing – preparing to launch her towards her ultimate panda future. How electrifying! She doesn't know where she's going to end up and how she's going to get there – she just knows that she has to move, so she can expand and reach for the stars – she can explode with panda-ness and light the world on fire! Bree is here to tell you that any future with you in it is always going to be bright and colorful and wonderful. Anything is possible – so seize the future. Seize it by believing in it right now. Seize it by recognizing the magic and vision that are coursing through your veins at this very moment. Seize it by letting your dream take hold of you and letting it grow in your space.

UNFURL YOURSELF LIKE A SHOOTING STAR

Whatever it is – a new project idea, a new journey, a new relationship, a new chapter in your story – you should cast it out far and wide – and let it pull you towards it! Soon, you'll see that you're just like a shooting star, unleashing stardust, sparkles and light out of your butt like you're farting a tail! Feel into your vision, download your potential, and grow into it! Grow into your bigger self – balloon your spirit up! Trust me, your body gets lighter when you have more soul-muscle to fire it up.

ALWAYS HEAD TOWARDS THE DIRECTION OF YOUR HEART

If you're lost in a pit of directionless despair and pessimism – like you're shouting into an endless void and being pulled into an abysmal dark (or you know, a lesser version of that kind of despair) – it is time to drink your coffee. Just kidding – it is time to check to see if you are really headed towards the direction of your coffee - HEART. Have you been chasing a ghostly shell, a false light that poses as your heart but really isn't? Have you been getting further and further away from your soul-fire? Time to turn towards the light - even if the future is a version of your life that blinds you and scares you a little! Don't be afraid - the future is always bright if you ignite it with your panda light!

Four of Wands

We are the Ferocious Four – we are strong because we recognize each other in our strengths. We are strong because we are a team (of four irresistibly adorable pandas)! #4everFam #SquadGoals #PandaPower

The pandas from the Four of Wands are family – and they refuse to be introduced separately or presented in any other light. They are really adamant about that and they are pawing my keyboard to make sure I get this passage right. Yes – they are a tightly bonded bunch. Are they related? You may ask. "Does it matter?" They will answer. "Family" – by blood, by choice or by circumstance – is family. It is a place of mutual belonging, acceptance, recognition and respect. It is a space where the four pandas celebrate and support each other – and it doesn't matter if one of them is napping or if the other one is curled up into a panda ball. It doesn't really matter what they're doing individually. They are pandas from the same tree. They are four pandas sharing a path, or a space together. In this particular chapter of their lives and on this particular spot of their journey, they have joined forces and banded together and chosen each other as "family". And they've got each other's backs.

YOU'RE SAFE!
YOUR FAM'S GOT YOU

Who is your family – both the one you are born into and the family you choose? Know that there are people in your life you can depend on, and there is always a place for you to feel safe and accepted. If you're unsure where that place is, look around! Your designated "fam" will patiently wait to give you a high-six (pandas have six fingers, just so you know), they will share the same vision as you, and they look forward to having you around just as much as you look forward to having them around.

DON'T BE A SACK OF POTATOES
IN A GROUP PROJECT

Expecting your fam to team-carry you and do all the heavy-lifting? You're not aspiring to be the one member that everybody dreads in a group project, are you? How come you're not tapping into your own potential, hmmm? How come you're still relying on others for their strengths, and not your own? The Fearsome Four Fire Pandas are looking at you a little funny right now. They don't understand why *you* don't see just how awesome and capable you are – if they're able to see it with their tiny panda eyes, why can't *you* see it? If they can so easily believe in you and what you can achieve, why can't you?

Five of Wands

GRAH!! Can we PLEASE do what I want?
What do you mean NO? That's preposterous.
Don't tell me what to do. You're not the boss of me!
BO-PING YOUR PAW IS IN MY FACE
AGAIN. Did you even wash it last night?
BLERGH!

Uh-oh, the pandas are stuck and collapsed on top of each other in a knot. As they struggle to break free from each other's Nelson holds, they stubbornly refuse to bend to each other's will. Stuck in a furry chaos with each panda wanting something different - competition and argument ensue. Sometimes it can be a good thing, since a messy panda spar is a great way to exercise your creative muscles and practice your footwork – requiring you to stand your ground while attempting to wrangle your "opponents", to find yourself amidst conflicting interests when no party is going to compromise. It's a great way to grow because it keeps you at the edge of your seat – a little positive pressure will help you sharpen into a panda diamond!

You have to be constantly moving, or you'll be knocked out! And if you happen to have weak ankles or a total lack of orientation in this fight, you'll also be knocked out! Or end up upside down, or have your face plastered against somebody else's butt. It's not the most pleasant scenario to test out your powers, but it can be exciting, experimental, and ultimately self-affirming. After all, if you can triumph over this panda knot or manage to walk away unscathed, you're really quite panda-tastic. (A quick shout-out to my artist, Celia, for coming up with the term "panda knot".)

YOUR HEROIC IDENTIFIER

What's your unique strength in a bout and a contest? Whatever it is, join the Panda Knot and let loose of your abilities. Try to untangle yourself from the wrestle-bustle! Don't be afraid of a confrontation – it's the perfect time to test your strength and work out your priorities!

> "Put a paw in their faces!" – a feisty panda

DEADLOCKED IN A FURRY PANDA KNOT

Sometimes, the best thing to do isn't to jam your fist into a face, trying to make way. Energy stirs up more energy, and an act of force will only attract an equally forceful reaction. Consider how you can keep calm and panda on to steer clear of this panda chaos!

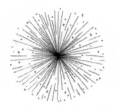

Six of Wands

Come - dinner awaits! I mean, uh, victory awaits!
Let us march with joy and pride in our stoma –
hearts. I mean hearts. Celebrate how far we've
come – and how far we shall continue to reach.
Strive, fellow pandas. Strive!

Jubilee is super excited and eager to move forward in life. Fellow pandas are lighting fireworks and sparklers for her in recognition of her achievements and her leadership, and they crown her with the laurels of victory for her distinguished vision and unwavering spirit. As you can see, she is not the type of panda to wait around for dinner. Oh sorry – she meant victory. I don't know why I typed dinner. She is always hungry...hungry for food, and hungry for glory! Jubilee is always on the move – always springing into action, always marching forward, and always leading by example and courage. Life isn't fun when she's not in the front, and life isn't meaningful when she's not pioneering into worlds unknown for her fellow pandas to witness. Not only is she manifesting and pursuing her own dreams – she is carrying the dreams and wishes of her panda tribe as well. They believe in her, after all. And she will not let them down.

THE WORLD NEEDS YOU TO LEAD, NOT FOLLOW

Has it ever occurred to you that maybe you don't really need someone to show you the way? And that you don't need permission to be unique, to go forward, to chase after what you want? Has it ever occurred to you that maybe you're the teacher that you're hoping to learn from, you're the champion to fight all the dragons and demons, and you are the answer to your questions? Has it ever occurred to you that maybe you don't need anyone else – but the world needs you instead?

IF YOU FALL, YOU'LL LAND ON SOMETHING SOFT

Maybe you're not one for the spotlight – and you get quite the stage fright. You probably don't want to trip, tumble down the stairs, and/or make a fool of yourself. Don't worry. The pandas understand – BUT, if you really think about it, pandas trip, tumble down hills and make fools of themselves all the time, don't they? They're still cute, aren't they? Who's ever made fun of a panda for trying or being silly? Nobody, that's what. So with that in mind - if you know just how cute you are, that's how cute you are. Unleash your inner panda! Even if you fall, you'll always land on your butt. That's the biggest cushion you have on your body, so there really isn't anything you need to worry about!

Jubilee insists on visiting you so she could give you her crown of victory in person. That's her at the door right now, not your Skip the Dishes – sorry not sorry. She's going to hand you her victory laurels. Because she thinks the world of you, duh. And of course you deserve it. You deserve everything and everything good in this beautiful world.

Seven of Wands

Oh, are you sure you want to have a go at me?
You do know pandas weigh up to 200 pounds,
right? We have A LOT of body mass available for
a good "sitting on" – if that is what you wish, don't
mind if I OBLIGE!

Rambo is taking a strong stance against the world. He's a rebellious panda, and the only panda will he follows is his own. His determination to stand against strong and dangerous opposition to maintain his own is admired by many – not a lot of pandas dare to do what he does. It takes courage and resolve to stand as a solo panda, to not surrender from pressure. Sometimes it's simply not enough to know what you want and want what you want. Sometimes you need to defend what you want in life. Sometimes you want one thing, but the world wants something different from you. Sometimes you need to brace yourself for impact so you can answer your calling. But you'll know in your heart when something is worth protecting. Your heart's desire, your fire and your inner light are always worth fighting for.

WHERE YOUR LINE AT?

What's something you're willing to defend with your paws? We all have something within us that is untouchable – something we will be willing to cast a ring of fire around to protect. If you draw this card – you are being tested! You're being called to show your suave moves! Everybody wants a stalk of your bamboo, and their paws may just inch closer and closer towards your treasure – it is up to you to say no! Name the things that are important to you, and decide that they aren't up for the taking!

HAVE YOU FORGOTTEN YOUR HERO NATURE?

Backed up in a corner and up against the wall? Nowhere to go, nowhere to run, and nowhere to hide? Um, can you not shoot fireballs out of your paw? Are you not the legendary panda that can produce a colossal chi-blast from your paw? The pandas know the exact kind of hero that you are, and that nothing is over until you say it is over! You can still turn the tide. You're a rock, a boulder, an unmovable mountain. You can do this!

Rambo wants you to know that he's up for hire if you need him to sit on the backs of your enemy and give them a good yin-yang.

Eight of Wands

Time to run, run, run! We shall be there to catch those stars when they land – and there's no time to waste! What do you mean you can't run that fast? Don't be silly. Didn't Victor lend you his bike, Rainbowburst? No excuses! The Universe is calling – and you must answer!

Sirius is not about that stylized sticks life – he insisted on making an appearance with shooting stars behind him, gliding across the sky. When your soul-fire is met with the bigger cosmic purpose and the currents of the universe – that's when your reality unfolds. These are the moments that take your breath away, the moments when we realize we are breaking into a little run so we can catch a star by its tail. Your dream is arriving, and it is within your grasp. But you gotta meet it halfway – the Universe gives no hand-outs! Sirius usually isn't too keen on running or exercising in general, but for this epic moment of magical manifestation, he shall make an exception. He has no excuse but to run. Otherwise, how will he ever catch his dreams? And being a total multitasker, he is packing his bamboo snacks so he can munch on them during his chase. Self-care *is* an important aspect of star-chasing, you know. You definitely don't want to starve yourself and run out of bamboo steam – especially when you're a panda.

TO INFINITY AND BEYOND

The world is an open bamboo forest, stretching towards infinity and beyond – pandas are free to feast as much as they want and grab as much as they can. All they need to do is to get there. Though you don't live in the Panda Kingdom and you may not necessarily like eating bamboo, the same universal law applies. Your world is equally abundant with opportunity – and it is up to you to seize them! What is calling out to you right now? Where is your heart telling you to go? Wish, and so it shall be. Dream, and become!

STOP WAITING AND DILLY-DALLYING. RUN!

Are you glaring at the night sky, watching shooting stars that land in other people's fields and wondering how come those sparkly cosmic gems aren't falling into your lap? Remember, the Universe can only meet you halfway! Action, reaction. Give, and receive. Cast your glance upon the night sky, and beckon your shooting star to come. And when it shows up, you better run with every single bit of your strength to meet it!

Nine of Wands

Unlike the fresh newbie Fire Pandas, I, Stryker, has a fur-ton of experience. After charging and rolling and tumbling butt-first into things all the time, you accumulate a certain degree of wisdom.

A panda in their defensive position always has their butt up – like Stryker, who guards the space in Nine of Wands. He's not quite sure if he should lower his legs to rest, curl up into a ball and roll some more, or take up his wand and let loose some "woo-pah's!" Catching a shooting star and chasing after a dream is a hard biz indeed, and sometimes a panda needs to be more strategic with his adorable advancing. If a panda isn't rolling, he can't be ballin'! But if he's rolling himself into head injuries all the time, then maybe he should be more cautious and take some time to figure out his next step. That's one of the reasons why he's keeping his butt up high – on one hand, he's distracting you with an unquestionable cute panda toosh – on the other hand, he is ready to roll whenever he feels ready!

BUILD YOUR FIRE
& SHINE IT ON ANOTHER DAY

It sucks when you roll butt-first into a challenge that slows down your momentum. It also sucks when you tumble your way into a dead-end, forcing you to take pause in order to strategize a timely detour in order to circumnavigate your adventures. Oh, how hard it is to be a Fire Panda! If you're a strong fire element, I'm sure you can relate to Stryker's predicament. But like he said, he's got a lot of experience and wisdom. He knows how to harness his fire and save it for another day when the time is more appropriate. What do you want to achieve right now? What's stopping you or inconveniencing you and forcing you to make a detour? How can you best save and manage your energy? What is the best route for circumnavigating your journey?

THE MUSCLE IS TENSE WHEN
THE WORLD IS OUT TO GET YOU

When a panda lifts up his buttocks for too long, he inevitably gets a little bit paranoid. What do you want from him? Are you trying to sabotage his success? Are you trying to steal from his treasures? Are you trying to lure him into wasteful merry-go-around ventures? What is it that you want!? If you find yourself grumping like Stryker on a bad day – take some time off so you can keep calm and panda on. What is the real source of your frustration and paranoia? How can you create more ease and flow? How can you best apply your experience and wisdom so that you can eventually move forward in the right direction? How can you "un-stuck" yourself and not have your adorable butt in the air all the time?

In case you didn't know, Stryker's favourite yoga move is the happy baby pose. When he's not intensely contemplating what he should do next and moping slightly over stunted efforts – he whips out a few happy baby rolls to keep himself limber. Why is he telling you this, you may ask? Well, the author needed a space filler so this page won't have a gaping text hole – but after a few rounds of editing and proofing, there turns out to be no gaping text hole at all, but this segment seems too fun to delete – so the author has chosen to keep it for your amusement.

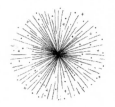

Ten of Wands

Ah, my panda brothers and sisters are lighting up the sky with fireworks. They're cheering for me. They're also saying something…lips are moving…paws are in the air…pand…zzzz….

zzzzzzzzzzzzzz…

Uh-oh, Cloude is out of commission. He's had a long day. I'm sure most of us can relate to him - exhaustion, overwhelm, backpains. Indeed, it is a struggle to be productive every day. We strive to stay on top of our game and sometimes we inevitably bite off more than we could chew. We get so stressed out by the responsibilities we shoulder and the obligations we take on, feeling so walled in and weighted down that we forget to take a break. Overwhelmed by the work he has done and the work that is yet to be done, Cloude decides that it is time to be a big pile of fur on top of a log. His paws are jello. His spirit is mashed potatoes. His fellow pandas, however, know how hard he's worked and are launching off fireworks into the sky to congratulate him on his progress and to cheer him on. Cloude isn't listening, however - he's already snoring! Tomorrow, when he wakes up, he'll be a better and stronger panda. But for now, he shall rest.

KEEP CALM AND NAP ON A LOG

We tend to encounter a Ten of Wands moment when we're trying too hard and forgetting that we're human. We've bitten off more than we could chew, and we take on obligations and responsibilities and shoulder realities that are too big for us. This either breeds muscle, or severe overwhelm. Despite our infinite god-nature and our manifesting powers – at the end of the day, we still occupy a human body that needs to eat and sleep. Cloude wants to give you (a super languid and lazy) paw-five to congratulate you on your resilience, and he offers you his napping log to rest on if you ever need to collapse and recharge with abandon.

I'M LOOKING AT YOU, YOU OVER-ACHIEVING WORKAHOLIC

Sometimes feeling overwhelmed can be a good thing – it means that you are creatively abundant, and you are inspired to achieve more in life. The desire to be more productive, more efficient and to get more work done – is a sign that you are striving. Having that said, there is a difference between striving and straining. Yes, I'm looking at you, you over-achieving workaholic and perfectionist. Your intense need to slay your monstrous to-do list or navigate your procrastination should not be an excuse to push your health into over-drive. What is the point of success and getting things done if you've got no "body" to "embody" that success? Take care of yourself. Or follow Cloude's example – take a nap.

Mm – what's that? Picture of Cloude for the 'gram, you said? Well, help yourself. He's completely conked out, but I don't think he will mind. Pandas are adorable no matter what they're doing. You better take a grass shot or protein kale smoothie before you approach, though. His sleep aura is very powerful. Here – take this pillow and hold it against your head, just in case.

Page of Wands

I'M READY! Let's go visit Solomon in his cave and annoy him! This is gonna be so amazing! Oh wait – I just remembered that there is a pandachelorette party somewhere – do you think we should go there instead? Ah!

Raiden is a curious explorer and is constantly distracted by – khem – I mean, *attracted* to new shiny things. She wants to see everything, smell everything, touch everything and do everything at the same time. All at once. Then move on to the next thing. Then the next. She also has the immense need to climb anything that is within her sight and within her paws reach - if it's got height and some gripping space, you bet she's going to climb it. This playful little rouge can be seen rolling and tumbling around the streets of Panda Kingdom, causing adorable trouble wherever she goes.

PANDA FOR HIRE

If you've been craving for some fresh experiences and you've dying to try something new, send Page of Wands an invitation because she loves a good party and a good party loves her! She'll help you reconnect with your fun-loving side, drag you (by your pants) out of your comfort zone and experience the world anew. She'll even lend you her adventurer's scarf if you give her a compliment. If she shows up at your door, you know it is time to shake things up a little and do something fun to celebrate life!

PANDA DISCLAIMER

Indeed, Page of Wands is an expert when it comes to having fun and living in the moment – however, you should know that she can be a little flaky and temperamental when she doesn't get what she wants. She doesn't want to wait around because waiting isn't fun! Because of that, she tends to shy away from taking up responsibilities and commitments, because she doesn't want to be tied down. Having fun and trying out new things is important, but if you know in your heart that you need to settle in order to deepen into an experience, you should probably take a rain-check with this jumpy panda before you get spirited away by her cute paws and charms!

Knight of Wands

Hey, you! Get your butt over here. I've got business with you…and I mean BIZnezz. And after we're done, let's go pick a fight with the Mad Boar, or exchange some paw-fists with our grizzly brothers!

Storm is the legendary, the one-and-only kung fu panda. Charismatic, fearless, and bold, Storm seeks the thrill of a good battle and spends his days hunting down worthy opponents to duel, rolling around town to rescue panda maidens in distress and wrestling fire-breathing dragons. It's never occurred to him that he can't beat something – his infectious confidence and perpetually boiling adrenaline inspire the pandas around him to pursue their goals with determination and fierce cuteness. This warrior panda's battle cries can be heard from miles away – usually followed by the sounds of trees smashing onto the ground, a myriad of explosions, or his enemy's pleas for mercy.

PANDA FOR HIRE

If you are on the verge of an epic quest, Storm is definitely the panda you want to call in for a magnificent courage boost. He'll grab your fear by the throat, axe-kick the limiting beliefs out of your system, and get your blood boiling and pumping for any upcoming adventures! He'll even help you work on your battle cry – he's *extremely* good at it.

PANDA DISCLAIMER

Indeed, sometimes to make progress in life – all we need is a few seconds of insane courage. The tiny steps that we take to push ourselves towards greatness are sometimes all that we need to create epic transformations in the way we live! HOWEVER, you should be careful with the Knight of Wands. Sometimes he gets too pumped up and his paw-fists unleash themselves without him even realizing. You should think twice before you decide if Storm is the panda you need to solve the issues at hand.

> "I NEED TO PUNCH SOMETHING." – Storm, the Knight of Wands

Queen of Wands

Life is like a sunflower, waking up to light every morning.

Always so full of sunshine and laughter, Abby is the ever-radiant Queen of Wands, a shining star full of warmth and light. The pandas that happen to meet her are always so bedazzled by her glorious aura. They are drawn to her because of the way she laughs: so genuine, so infectious and so full of life. Pandas big and small follow her around, hoping to spend some time with her, to catch her attention, to listen to her story, to watch her savor whatever she is doing with honesty and fullness. They want to be inspired by her, loved by her, entertained by her. And she never disappoints. When you smile in her presence, it is always a smile from the depths of your soul - a cosmic sunflower that blooms and blossoms from within. Of course – she is the Queen of Wands – the Queen of Fire. The Queen of Life. The dancing diva that dives headfirst into the centre your heart – and re-emerging (in slow motion, fur catching the rays of the sun) – exploding and enveloping you with joy and beauty and light.

PANDA FOR HIRE

Queen of Wands is a free spirit, always brimming with life. She *loooves* life. The fact that she's breathing. The fact that she can follow her heart and go wherever she pleases. The fact that there is so much joy and adventures to be had. Absolutely and wholeheartedly she loves life. If you need to be reminded of your own vitality, your own light and your own beauty – invite Abby into your life. She won't do your bidding for you, but she will infect you with her passion for self-expression and inspire you to be boldly yourself and no one else. You'll resonate with her – not because she is a magical panda with special powers to ignite one's thirst for life. You'll resonate with her because you, too, is a queen and burns just as brightly and gloriously.

PANDA DISCLAIMER

A light dose of rule-breaking and playful abandon is good for the soul from time to time – sometimes we just need to remember to live to our fullest potential, and to express without a care in the world – because when we do so, we inspire others and give them permission to do the same. Having that said, Queen of Wands can sometimes be too much of a free spirit. There are times when she ends up "blinding" others with her "light". She can be intense, self-centred, and guilt-trippy when you're not sharing her optimism or enthusiasm. She gets bummed out when you're not enjoying life to the fullest with her – unable to respect or understand that sometimes people need space to process their experiences and emotions on their own time. When you find yourself going overboard with Queen of Wand's energy, just remember a queen's essence is to love and nurture. You honor your own light but do not forget to honor the light of others. It only gets brighter when everyone is shining together.

King of Wands

Cuteness explosion – UNLEASH! Ultimate furry powers, UNLEASH! Magnificent manifestation, UNLEASH! My flaming panda kingdom, UNLEASH!

I know what you're thinking – he kind of looks like a colorful ghost, or some kind of legless apparition! In a sense, that's who Blaze is. He's a little mind-bending, a little dream-like – because he's the panda that everybody looks up to. He's a furball of pure manifesting power, a visionary, a dream machine. Whatever he thinks, he achieves. If he can see it, he can create it. He's the centrepiece, the adorable convergence of all the creative energies in the universe. He's the panda channel that converts ethereal particles into physical form. So you see, he's more than just a regular panda. Not only is he an embodiment of his own panda visions, he is also the vision, the source of inspiration, the success story that other pandas strive towards.

That's why he's a bit of an apparition. That's why he's a bit of a demi-god panda. He's the frigging King of Wands.

PANDA FOR HIRE

Blaze is your go-to panda for manifesting galactic visions and sparkling dreams. Nothing is impossible in his panda mind – you pitch an idea to him – he will amplify it a thousand times back at you. He'll believe in it so much that you will believe in it, too. There will be doubt in your mind, in your body, in your soul. He'll convince you that you are the perfect vessel for your dreams, and the things you dream are always within your reach. So dare to dream big with the King of Wands – because nothing is too big for the King of Wands!

PANDA DISCLAIMER

Blaze carries dreams and visions that are bigger than himself. That is his power, but it can sometimes be his downfall. He commits to being a vessel and channel for his ideas. A lot of times he pursues his visions at the expense of everything else that he deems "less important" – such as his health or his relationships. Sometimes he even loses himself in the process, and he certainly doesn't see the harm in that. Be careful when you invite the King of Wands to join your manifesting team. His intensity is infinitely propelling, but can also be smothering if you don't balance it with other types of panda presence.

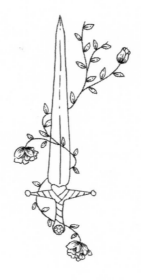

SUIT OF SWORDS

The Air Pandas

The Air Pandas await your attendance with a cup irresistible bamboo tea – these adorable brainiacs are ready to jump in whenever you are trying to get to the bottom of things, or whenever you are seeking the truth and a logical solution. Do not underestimate these bears – they are tough, caffeinated minds that never lose their *bearings* no matter how dire the situation becomes.

Life is an open school,
a quest for knowledge and truth

Air Pandas see life as a journey towards greater learning and self-betterment. They are constantly thirsty for interesting information and new knowledge, eagerly exploring and considering new ideas. Anything that will add to their understanding, challenge their current perspective and expand their mental horizons is exciting and rewarding for them. Almost always, you can find the nerdy pandas from the Air Panda Kingdom crowding the local libraries, bending their cute heads over bamboo scrolls and burying their curious noses in between dusty pages or sandwiching themselves between leather-bound hardcovers. When Air Pandas aren't pawing their way through ancient manuscripts or databases, they can be seen having passionate discussions with each other, engaging in a rigorous contest to see which panda is louder – I mean, khem-khem, partaking in *lively debates* and testing out ideas to see which ones stand.

These posh pandas' got an attitude!

The Air Pandas are natural philosophers and thinkers with a passion for deep introspection and the cultivation of intelligence. Do not be fooled by their nerdy glasses, fuzzy scarves and *aww*-inducing bowties though – these are definitely not pandas you want to take lightly! The Pandas of the Air Kingdom will always give you their piece of mind and are never afraid to express themselves with their powerful panda voice. If you see an Air Panda, you bet that panda is talking. Although it is a truth universally acknowledged that Air Pandas *love* being listened to more than anything else – they encourage you to speak up and project your voice because they love a fellow thinker and speaker to contend themselves with! As mentioned before – they *love* a good debate and they love it *even more* when their opponents are as strong and opinionated as they are. Seeing that you are reading this book, they told me to tell you that they are eager to hear from you and learn about your unique perspective about yourself and the world. You are free to say whatever you want to say – but just a tiny heads-up: do not, under any circumstances, touch their coffee, unless you want to release a panda storm.

YOU CAN CALL ON THE AIR PANDAS FOR THEIR HIGH IQ IF YOU ARE:

☼ Looking to bond over a casual but stimulating conversation as well as a cup of caffeinated beverage

☼ Planning to embark on a quest for knowledge and better understanding

☼ Needing to awaken some brain muscle to tackle a difficult decision or problem

☼ Needing to give someone a piece of your mind and establish some boundaries

☼ Wanting to explore your identity, your worldview and your unique perspective through active self-reflection and panda pondering

☼ Seeking to strengthen and project your unique voice and express your thoughts unapologetically

☼ Manifesting some attitude because, why not!

PONDERING PANDA

☼ What's something that you know about yourself that won't change – even if the Air Pandas are feisty toward you in a debate?

☼ What is something that you have strong opinions about – something that gets your mind racing 200 miles per hour as if it's been fueled by gallons of caffeine? Why?

☼ What do you do to make sense of your thoughts and your experiences? Air Pandas love to externalize their thoughts in any way possible – their favourite thing to do is to unleash the bits and bobs of their mind upon an unsuspecting victim, usually a Water Panda.

Activating Your Inner Air Panda: A Ritual for Speaking Your Truths

Read and recite this passage for an instant Air Panda Power Boost. For the moments when you are wrought with uncertainty and doubt – this prayer will help you find your mental grounds and let you know where you stand. You can also recite this passage to strengthen and amplify a truth or resolve that you already have.

You know the truth of who you are. You have always known. You know it now, and you will know it to be true no matter what the future holds. Now write it down, with ink and paper. With feather and light. Carve it onto the pages of your story, the truth that shall guide you through the darkness, the miasma, the labyrinths of life. The world is spinning, a storm is sending shocks to your core. You could disintegrate. You could cease to exist and become nothing. You could disappear into the void, never to be seen again.

You feel into your truth: it is unshakable, unquestionable, non-negotiable. It is your anchor. Your sword. Your backbone. You will write it as you make history. You will speak it – let it ring through your throat. The storm rages on, smothering your voice. But your words cut through this flying disaster like a clear, crystal blade. The Air Pandas emerge. They form a protective circle around you, shielding you from the rain and the thunderous cries of oppression. They touch you with their paws and raise their swords towards the sky, channeling your words through their body and blasting them upwards, blasting the heavens open, parting the clouds of chaos.

And you speak. Your voice soars and pierces through the atmosphere. The Air Pandas are cheering you on and crying your name, repeating your message and tearing the sky open. Together, you watch the colors of the galaxy pour in from the gateway that you've opened – cosmic birds cascading and spiraling downwards, descending, and flying towards you. You welcome them as they dive into your mouth – grounding you, affirming you, transforming you, uplifting you.

You open your mouth, and light bursts forth. You speak. You declare. You make yourself known. This is your truth. This is your truth that shakes and anchors and makes the world. This is who you are.
This, is who you are.

Ink Bottles, Writing Feathers and Panda Paws

This spread is for when you need to break free from attitudes and mindsets that have shackled and caged you – when you need to write a new story…with the possible assistance from the Air Pandas.

1. **The Heavy Prison Ball.** What limiting belief chains you at your ankles, preventing you from being your truest and most authentic self?

2. **Splattered Ink in Your Heart.** Why does it still hold power over you? How did this blotched spot come to exist on your page?

3. **Air Pandas Take a Look.** Sorry to interrupt this spread – but Air Pandas are quite nosy when it comes to helping their designated human. They will read your manuscript and give

you their completely neutral feedback. For this position: what do the Air Pandas think of your experience and circumstance?

4. **Air Pandas Give You Feedback.** Sorry, sorry – they are still here. I can't get them to stop talking. For this position, the Air Pandas will give you suggestions on how you can improve your story and make it better.

5. **A Thousand Second Chances.** The Air Pandas return your story pages. You look at the blotched ink spot (as well as the scribbled panda footnotes), and you draw a flower on top. How can you transform your story into an empowering one?

6. **A New Draft.** The Air Pandas are excited to see what you will write next. What have you learned from your past experiences and your fears? What themes are you able to extract to serve the story you want to write now? What is your truth that you shall use to guide your future narrative so that you will always write stories that are your own?

7. **Bonus Position: The Air Pandas are Still Talking and They Won't Leave You Alone.** What can I say...they are really invested in how your story is going to turn out! If you still want to hear from these helpful, smarty-pants pandas and receive additional advice and panda wisdom from them – pull one more card to indulge them!

Ace of Swords

Always know the truth of things, especially the truth of yourself. That way, you can't be bothered by idiots, or idiots that say idiotic things. Also, you must always remember to wear a bowtie. Such fashion is needed to protect your throat chakra.

Arry is one of the leading philosophers and thinkers in the Air Panda Kingdom. He teaches at the University of Pandas, receiving over seventy-eight academic awards for his extensive and outstanding research on human behavior and the archetypal symbolism of the tarot system. He is proud of his academic work and enjoys teaching and sharing his knowledge with others. When he's not "broadcasting" his innovative ideas and discoveries about the human condition, he can be seen sharpening his precious sword collection and adjusting his polka-dot bowtie – as well as engaging in a dance of wit with his fellow Air Pandas that think themselves smart enough to challenge him.

PARDON THE INTERRUPTION

Power comes from knowing yourself from within and out. Our lives are guided by our actions, and our actions are guided by our thoughts, and our thoughts are guided by our perception and understanding of the world around us. Therefore, to seek a better life, we must seek better actions. To seek better actions, we must seek better thoughts. To seek better thoughts, we must –

Arry, please give me back my keyboard.

NO. This is my card. I must ensure all necessary messages are conveyed in the upmost clarity and intelligence. Just because you are the author doesn't mean you are entitled to write this book all by yourself!

PLEASE CARRY ON

I apologize for the intrusion. No, this is not Kim, the author. This is Arry, and I will be writing my own panda power-up, thank you very much. Now – where were we? Ah, yes. To seek better thoughts, we must seek to understand how we perceive and understand the world, for that is the core of our identity – the matrix of memories, values, opinions and ideas that inevitably shape us. We -

Can you at least help me pose some thoughtful questions so my readers can self-reflect?

QUESTIONS FOR REFLECTION

Don't tell me what to do – I was just getting to that! Ah, yes, indeed. What makes *you* who you are? What opinions do you have – what kind of subject matter interests you? How do you define right and wrong? How do you define love? How do you define yourself? What made you think the way you do and act the way you do? What made you who you are now? How can you use your knowledge to navigate your life towards the promised eternal darkness, the futile accumulation towards no – *alright, alright I'll stop! I was merely joking about the cold empty void of nihilism. Life is wonderful. So full of meaning!*

Two of Swords

Ah, so many considerations - I don't know what I will choose. I do know I need more tea, however. Yes, tea. English Breakfast with soy coffee cream and a paw of sugar. Not a full paw – sheesh. I'm not a savage.

As you can probably tell, Hugo likes to mull things over...A LOT. He's always on the verge of a breakthrough, testing multiple theories and engaging in thought experiments to solve whatever puzzle or conundrum he is stuck on. This doesn't bother him much, though. Unlike humans, pandas don't feel pressed to make a decision quickly and the thought of not arriving at an immediate conclusion for a period of time doesn't really bother them. Hugo is especially so. Thinking, considering, exploring or mulling things over helps him strengthen his critical thinking muscles. Most importantly, all these mental exercises keep him on his metaphorical toes and help him know himself better. He is a "processing machine" and he doesn't mind spending time to make sure the answer is correct, accurate and true.

TIME TO SHARPEN YOUR CRITICAL THINKING SKILLS

There's no such thing at a mental still-mate. If you don't know what to think, then perhaps you're not doing it right. It's not really about "what" you think – it's about "how" you think. How can you process the information you have and understand the situation better? What are some of the perspectives that you have not yet considered? Don't be afraid or frustrated when you can't seem to find the answer right away. You *will* find the answer and there are many different ways to approach the same problem. *You're* in control. You get to compare and analyze ideas to see if they are useful or not. As you examine your options and explore your thoughts about each one, you will come to know your priorities and your principles. Such is the quest for truth!

STILL AT THAT STILLMATE?

If you are, unfortunately, trapped in a still-mate – it is perhaps a sign that you have done all the thinking that you can. Time to get off your panda buttocks and spring to action! Do something. Anything. Flip a coin if you absolutely can't decide. Or don't decide. Go for a walk to change up the energy and generate some flow. Do some downward dogs and stretch out your back and your hamstrings. Browse the internet for some adorable panda memes. Take a break and resume your mental anguish – I mean, uh, the tug-o-war of thoughts – later when you feel refreshed and rejuvenated!

Three of Swords

Reality is harsh; it is hard to look at – but I must turn my gaze towards it…for this is the price of truth. P.S. I am not dead: just resting with a book on my back that I uh, stabbed. Just so done with the world, really. I don't care anymore!

Contrary to popular belief, Clover is not dead. She's a little melodramatic with the things she finds immediately unsettling. Like the book she was reading, for example. She was unexpectedly confronted with something so shocking and distorting that her sense of self and reality shattered a little. Out of anger, resentment and grief, she stabbed the covers with three swords and now she's draped herself over a tree stump, making a total scene. As she hangs with her limbs loose and helpless, her favourite glasses break and fall to the ground. Everything seems to be happening in slow motion. And of course, to top it off, it is raining. Cue sad violin. Whatever.

Fine by her. Nothing to see here – just a panda with a broken worldview and a bleeding soul. Shoo, shoo.

WE KNOW NOT WHAT WE KNOW

Three of Swords is a shocking moment of contradicting realities clashing towards each other – and being unable to compromise or co-exist – they break and cause damage. Our beliefs are questioned and perhaps invalidated. We no longer have a grasp on what we think we know. The world is changing. The grounds of reality are shifting. What we knew to be true no longer stands, and it is quite possible that we get swallowed up by this chasm that is opening up in our consciousness. What do we do? What would *you* do? What was something you learned that challenged you so deeply that you felt you could no longer trust what you know? What is something difficult you have to go through where there is no right or wrong answer – where there's no clear guide on how you should think or act?

LIFE IS SAD AND COMPLICATED

If you need to cry – you should. Unleash those tears. Release the kraken. Swim in the salty lake of your sorrows and woes. And then, slowly but surely, you'll drift towards shore. Acknowledge your Three of Swords moment and be at peace with the fact that it is alright to *not* have a straightforward answer. Know that sometimes the answer isn't black and it isn't white – it may be red like blood, and it may be gray and bleak as rain. Clover has certainly gone through her share of soul-shattering moments – but nothing has managed to stop her from continuing to trust and pursue her truths thus far. Seriously, nothing. I know she's totally making a scene earlier, but you should see what she always does afterwards. Guess how many swords she is carrying on her back now? That's right, three. And she's already shopping for a new pair of glasses on Pamazon.

If you ever need to shop on Pamazon, Clover has premium discount codes for being a Prime member – make sure you hit her up before you commit to any major shopping!

Four of Swords

Mmm, sorry – what did you say? Oh, these swords over here? I'm just collecting my thoughts. I haven't decided what I'm going to do with them yet.

First of all, Quinn loves her bean bag; it's practically her second brain and she can't think without it. These two are inseparable and are often seen pondering side by side next to each other. Or rather, stacked on top of one another, depending on the time of day. She loves to be alone with her thoughts – she often arranges her collection of ideas neatly on the floor, all laid out before her, so she can look at them and observe them clearly. When she's tired of contemplating, she falls asleep and dreams about catching books with fluttering wings levitating overhead or solving riddles in front of ancient Sphinxes. Sometimes, she puts on her glasses so it may look like she's concentrating on some serious thought – but in truth, she's all but closed her eyes and dozed off while maintaining a studious air. Not that you can see her eyes, anyway. Pandas have camouflage-grade eye fur – one of the reasons why panda professors can never tell who's sleeping and who isn't in the classroom. Anyway - introspection is hard work, y'all. A panda must sleep in order to think properly. Yes, indeed.

YOU SHOULD MIND THE BREAK

Quinn is one of the "chillest" pandas in the Air Panda Kingdom. She's always cool, calm and collected and never rushes into a decision or an opinion. She takes her time to organize her thoughts and to relax her mind when she needs to. She knows that humans have the tendency to get lost in a mental frenzy and are extremely anxiety-prone – so she's offering you her bean bag to rest your brains whenever you need it. What are some tell-tale signs that you tend to experience when you are mentally spiraling out of control? When do you usually find yourself needing a break and what do you do to "take your mind off things"?

OR...YOU SHOULD PROBABLY STOP ZONING OUT

On the other hand – are you *too* comfortable resting on that beanbag? Are you zoning out until your eyes are out of focus, drowning the noises of the world and refusing to engage, and sleeping through the fire? Is your brain feeling like dead meat right now? If you are one or all of the above – it is time to stop drooling and covering your ears with "la-la-la's"! Gather your thoughts – one at a time, and reengage with the world! If your mind is sleeping, then who's driving the car on this grand cosmic road trip of life!? Well, certainly not you. Maybe the zombie you, or worse – someone else! Quinn is pinching you on the cheek and is getting ready to swing for a slap. You best snap yourself awake before that paw reaches you.

Five of Swords

Yes, I said it! According to my perfectly structured, perfectly logical and perfectly informed opinion, your glasses. Are. UGLY.

It's difficult to tell – but Kiki and Nester are actually best friends. Their intellectual rivalry started out in their childhood: one of them championed coffee as the chosen deity of caffeinated drinks, while the other deemed any beverage that doesn't come from a sachet of loose leaves and steaming water can be considered utter garbage. Their relentless arguments and fervent debates last to this day. I know, I know – it looks like they are at each other's throats all the time, but these two pandas have nothing but respect for each other. The fact that they have yet to settle this caffeinated conundrum proves that they are worthy of each other's wit and mental reflexes – and these two pandas won't have it any other way.

DO YOU REALLY KNOW
WHAT YOU THINK YOU KNOW?

The Air Pandas are never afraid to have their opinions or worldviews challenged. They may dread it and resent it from time to time (usually when they lose the argument) but for the most part, they welcome a healthy debate and an occasional petty mental showdown. It keeps their fluffy brains well exercised and well-toned. Facing and tackling a difficult opinion or a different mental stance can be an incredible opportunity to locate your assertiveness, or an awesome way to explore where you are currently positioned in the world. Are you right, or are you wrong? Is there more to discover, unravel and unlock? Is there more to learn? Are your perspectives valid? Or perhaps they are underdeveloped? Or maybe you are misinformed and you didn't even know...or maybe you have been right all along?

QUIET IS NEEDED FOR MY SANITY

Kiki and Nester take turns when they go at each other. One of the pandas is toppled over right now, but he stood victor the other day and was proud. If you find yourself constantly being shoved to the floor with mouth screaming and shouting at your precious face, then take this card as your permission to yell "SHUT UP!" It's not a debate when the other party doesn't follow the rules. It's not a friendly mental sparring when one person decides to infringe and insult. Oh, and it certainly isn't heated conversation when someone is literally shredding your personal space and refusing to partake in any exchange. Sometimes you need to put your paw down by saying something unpleasant – do it. It's for the greater good.

Six of Swords

The paper boat carries the haiku of my thoughts as cherry blossom petals gently fall. Oh, where is it headed – and where, oh where will it go?

Takeshi is by the river. He's come to the banks of this river many times, and many times he leaves and each time is his last. The river is never the same; it is always changing, shifting in colors and texture. Sometimes he tries to catch his own reflection in the water, as the ripples and currents reveal to him, beyond his vision, a secret world. Each time he comes to this river to say goodbye to something: a bad habit, a memory, a lover, an old way of life. He bids them farewell as his thoughts course down the river with the currents of the water, and each time the sunlight will catch and shimmer and glisten on the flowing surface – a wink from his angels, or a hello from the Universe, perhaps.

SLOWLY BUT SURELY,
WE DRIFT TOWARDS SHORE

Oftentimes in life we know that we are leaving something behind. There is this feeling of anticipation. We keep standing on tiptoes to look ahead, but we are not sure what we are looking at or what we are searching for. One way or another, we have arrived at this point of spaciousness – our mind reaching for something in the distance – looking far beyond the horizon, hoping to see – what do we hope to see? A ship? A bird? A message in the bottle – or shore? We don't know, but we know that if we drift long enough – we will find something, or something will find us. Something exciting – something dreadful – or something boring? We don't know, but one thing is for sure: it will be different from what we have now. All we need to do is observe…and wait.

JUST BECAUSE YOU'RE A
SAGITTARIUS

When we wander with purpose, when we know there is something that we need to find – even when we don't know what it is – we are moving forward. We are making progress even when the roads criss-cross and meander. It's dangerous to move without the intention of finding something – if you're not trying to get anywhere – does that mean you're lost without direction? Does that mean you are trying to get…nowhere? Takeshi, being the wise and thoughtful panda that he is, has written a message on a piece of paper and folded it into a paper crane. It's for you, of course. An invitation for you to visit him by the river he frequents. If you don't know where to go or what you're waiting for, the two of you can go river-watching together. And who knows – maybe a paper boat will surface, and it, too, will carry your thoughts and reveal to you where you should be headed next.

Cherry blossom dreams
Paper boats and bamboo leaves
Never to return

— Takeshi

Seven of Swords

What's the fun in staying the same? The world needs a rebel like me, so new ideas can be born. ARRRRRRRRR! What, you don't agree? That's fine by me – as long as I agree with myself, I can go anywhere I please!

Jack Parrow is the noble rebel – or so he likes to think of himself. Not one for rules, rigid thinking and boring old systems – he likes to do things out of the box, out of the blue, and out of order. He is quite happy with himself as the star of his own show, and doesn't care if he sticks out like a sore thumb. The other pandas gawk at his infamous ingenuity – some with admiration and some with distaste. Not all of his ventures become inspirational stories of heroism. Some of them become cautionary tales that mother pandas use to curb their young cubs of bratty behavior, but some of the details of his daring conquests do strike people as innovative and energizing. Indeed, sometimes Jack Parrow may end up being wrong or making a mess even for himself– but that is the way he chooses to live. He's always on the edge. Always non-conforming. Always taking a little risk and causing wide-eyed exclamations or furrowing brows. He's a free spirit and a handsome pirate, and he shall never live otherwise.

ROBIN HOOD, BUT PANDA

Don't worry – Jack Parrow isn't coming to steal your stuff. Not yet, anyway! Just kidding. He will never! (You should check your deck collection.) Seriously, he is here to help you and will never touch your things without your permission (seriously, you should check that special edition that you went through great pains to acquire). Other than gunning for your precious deck collection (maybe), Jack is also here to challenge you to a duel. Didn't expect that – did you? THINK FAST! And dodge his cutlass! Never settle into your routines – *slash!* – always challenge yourself with new ideas – *clang!* – and do something that's never done before! – *deadlock!* – and NEVER. GIVE. UP. *Jack maneuvers your sword with a twist, sending it into the air. He catches it with his free paw. He smirks, and hand you back your sword. "Now, again!"*

ARRRRRRRRRRRRRRRR!
RULES ARE RULES

You may have noticed: Jack Parrow is a pirate. Indeed, he's a mischievous lawbreaker that is quite pleased with himself – always charming the girls and winning hearts all over with that adorable smirk of his. But beware – sometimes it's fun to break the rules, but when it comes to following necessary instructions and doing actual hard work – you don't want this thiefy panda to be your partner in crime. He's gonna tell you to cut corners, stray off the proper path and "steal" for results. Whatever it is you're trying to "steal"...be it time, resources or success – it's not going to end well. You don't need to follow any rule that does not ultimately benefit you, your process or your personal journey, but you should definitely have principles in place to help you stay on course – *proper* course.

Eight of Swords

UGHGUHGUH
uhgughuHGGUHGUHGUHghughUGHGUH. I
can't do this. I can't do this anymore – this is too
hard. What if I fall and shatter my cute head?
What if those swords cut me? What if I can never
get down? Oh no, what if I lose my grip!? What if
there are monsters in those dark clouds? What if
this is forever? AHHHHHHHHH!

Dorothy spends a lot of time in her head. To be fair, she does have the tendency to get caught up in sticky situations that are extremely anxiety and stress-inducing – and sometimes she forgets that she's actually a nimble ninja panda with a quick wit and agile limbs. That's kind of just how she is though – her thoughts speed and pick up and escalate into a whirlwind, spiraling out of control and swallowing all rationality and logic.

During those moments, she becomes disoriented by the chaos and the frenzy and the drama. However, as soon as she remembers that there's nothing she can't handle if she tackles one thing at a time, her vision refocuses, her heartbeat steadies and her brain immediately begins to churn with potential solutions to her problems. Yes, the terrain is dangerous. The swords may cut her if she lets go of the branch and falls, but if she stays close to the trunk of the tree and slides down slowly with a firm grip, she can come out of this situation perfectly unharmed – perhaps a few scrapes and scratches here and there, but once she's on the ground, she can inch her way out of this fence of sharp edges carefully. And voila! She'll be a free panda in no time.

A CURSE AND A BLESSING - BUT MOSTLY A BLESSING

Dorothy will tell you that having an extremely detail-driven mind that swarms and mobilizes and races 500 miles per hour is both a curse and a blessing. If you're like her and you constantly find yourself in stressful and anxious situations where you can't stop thinking about all the bad things that will happen – acknowledge that you are feeling disoriented and maybe even a little helpless. You got this. Here's the beauty of being worry-prone – it makes you extremely cautious and thorough. If you have the brainpower to spiral out of control with every single doomsday thought that is known to pandakind, this clearly means you have the exact same amount of brainpower available at your disposal to help you navigate those disasters, real or imaginary, with preventative measures and practical solutions. Your brain strains and strives with information – it helps you stay safe and prepared.

PROBLEM SOLVE LIKE A BOSS

Hey, look! Dorothy is on the ground already. She turns her body sideways and slides out of the fence of swords one step at a time, being mindful of her belly and taking great care to suck it in. She dips her paw into the dark clouds – just miasma from the swamp underneath – not a bottomless pit of death. Not exactly pleasant, but better than she anticipated. Oh, she's waving at you and making her way across the swamp towards you! You best meet her halfway – she has a message for you.

MESSAGE FROM MS. NEUROTIC BEAR

"Sometimes your mind can be a crazy place – a place not even caffeine can reach and help solve! Don't give in to the pessimistic and apocalyptic naggings. Terrible things can and do happen, but with every decision that you make to stay on top of your game, you will learn how to navigate fearful situations with more skill and confidence. You will learn to depend on the strengths you do have and you will discover what are the real threats you are facing and what are the imaginary ones that needn't concern you. You got this!"

With that, Dorothy hands you a raven feather – it is dark and regal and beautiful. Ah, that was why she climbed that tree in the first place. A token of her friendship and her blessings, for you.

Nine of Swords

There are monsters in the closet - but I shall face them bravely. Come out, monster! Here you are! Ah, it is my old unwashed sock from ten years ago - how ghastly. Oh and a green-horned demon with creepy hands - surprise, surprise. Oh, never mind. It's just my mother-in-law. Actually, I do mind. Apparently, she's read what I've written and she's going to murder me now. Good-bye, everyone. It's been a pleasure. See you in the afterlife.

Don't worry, Steve is still very much alive. He does have a bruise on his cheek from a session of "brutal" pinching, however. All things considered, it wasn't as bad as he had imagined – although he did feel like he was being consumed by a dark chasm of harsh winds and doom when his mother-in-law loomed closer and closer towards him. He thought he was going to be gutted alive then roasted on a bamboo pike. What a nightmare! But he's happy that he stood his ground – he stared fear in the eye, he did! Other than his mother-in-law, he prides himself for being able to withstand any sort of haunting – ghosts, fire ants, rotten bamboo salads, and the miscellaneous terrors of life. Many times, he's been in the bellies of the monsters he's tried to fight, mentally preparing himself to accept his tragic fate of cycling through the digestive tracks of cosmic oblivion. During those times – he remembers: *This is not what I'm made of!* And he punches his way free out of the beast's stomach and lands on the floor with a cute pose. Or, his lovely wifey puts a gentle paw on his back and tells him that he's snoring too loudly and she has a long day tomorrow. Either way, he rises from his nightmares, and adjusts his pillows.

BUMMER – DEMONS GALORE! BUT SO ARE ANGELS

Despair is almost always a certainty when it comes to living and breathing – the demons in our mind never rest, do they? But remember, demons aren't the only things that live in our mind. There are angels too: healers and brave warriors, beings of pure love and steel. Monsters are real, but so are heroes – heroes like you. Heroes with the kind of mental fortitude to take on colossal titans and giants of the old world. Heroes that face their fears with their knees knocking against each other and their souls trembling at the horrible sights they have to behold. Heroes that keep going despite having their hearts turned cold. Indeed, monsters are real. But aren't you a courageous juggernaut that stops at nothing? Or have you forgotten that?

YOU ARE SUPPORTED AND LOVED (EVEN WHEN THAT LOVE IS SERVED WITH SASS)

Monsters are everywhere. Sometimes we look them in eye to realize that they aren't real, and sometimes we pick up a sword to fight and conquer them. Remember that you never have to do this alone, there are also times where we can rely on the healing comfort and warmth of a familiar paw. Steve's wife has a streak of sass when her husband is spasming with self-induced melodrama, but when he's truly backed up in a corner and surrounded by wolves, she never hesitates to stand by his side, defending him and offering her unconditional love and support to her favourite panda in the whole wide world.

Ten of Swords

This cannot be…oh it simply cannot be…but one must shed the hairy layers of one's identity…to be fluffily reborn. IT HURTS THOUGH. IT REALLY HURTS. It feels like someone is ripping patches of my fur off with gorilla tape while pouring lemon juice and wasabi down my nose. Honestly, what could be worse!?

Hector is experiencing a tremendous moment: he's shedding his old skin. It has been a painful realization to notice that the part of him that he'd been carrying – the aspect of his identity that he thought to be real and thus deeply treasured – was no longer serving him. As soon as he realizes, he notices that a zipper appears at his back, followed by an insane itch. He knows that he needs to take it off soon – or this oversized ego onesie will smother him and take him alive. How has he come to endure this fake skin – that barely even resembled him anymore – for so long? Doesn't matter now. He's leaving. He looks at the mirror one last time, and stares at his own image that is no longer the truth of who he is. The mirror shatters. He's ready – and he takes hold of that zipper with his paw, with a rush of courage, he unzips his body, baring his true soul. Years of stuffing and cotton burst forth, and he steps out of his old skin. Now, he is brand new, and closer to himself than he's ever been.

TAKE OFF THAT EGO ONESIE: IT'S THE WRONG SIZE FOR YOU AND YOU DON'T LOOK CUTE IN IT.

If you're still looking at the card and wondering if Hector is still there – look no further, because he's not there anymore. He left a long time ago. He left because he had to – he needed to leave his old self behind in order to live more freely, more authentically. For the longest time, he could not let go of his past – sometimes it felt like he was forced to change, and that things happened to him against his will. Sometimes it felt like he carried the world's weight on his back and he was punctured by ten merciless swords, pinning him to the ground, refusing to let him move. But in the end, it wasn't him that those swords pinned down. His soul, unlike his body, was and remains light as a feather. And though part of him didn't want to leave it behind, he knew it was for his highest good. So with great effort, he did. And now he asks you: what is the part you that you know is smothering you and no longer serving you? What is a memory, an experience, or a relationship that holds so much gravity and so much negative weight that is stopping you from being the best that you can be? It shall be easy to find, because it'll be the most difficult thing you'll ever have to leave behind.

MIRROR, MIRROR ON THE WALL

Hector offers you a gift: it's his broken mirror. No, it's not for you to look at yourself. He knows that most of us don't need to be reminded of the part of our identity that we ourselves refuse to look at. You don't need to look at it, because it doesn't matter how you appear to be or how the world perceives you. It's not about what you look like, it's about what you think you look like. To transcend your ego onesie, you must learn to look within and connect or reconnect with the spirit of yourself that is always radiant beauty and freedom. It's the part of you that you will always know to be real. It will hurt a little – or it will hurt a lot. But it's like a workout. You may end up hating every minute of it when you are in the throes of it, but once your muscle soreness subsides, you will feel how strong that you have become.

Page of Swords

Animals with the Cute Gene accumulate more views on Youtube, and are known to lower stress and promote long-term happiness.

Bailey is the token nerd of the Air Panda Kingdom – she frequents the libraries and ancient panda archives, thirsty to explore interesting questions to satiate her intellectual curiosity. She thinks quite highly of herself (but just the right amount – with a little extra) – as all Air Pandas do – and she can be a little snobby when it comes to fact-checking others. When she's not burying her nose in library books, you can find her cocking her head in an adorably questioning and slightly condescending manner to signal her disapproval and her superiority in knowledge. Despite that, she is also easily impressed and loves it when you can tell her something that she doesn't know. She'll be quite salty at first because she still likes to think that she's the smartest panda in the universe who is on her way to ultimate greatness – but only a little. Her passion and curiosity for new information, new perspectives and new knowledge overrides any pretentiousness and arrogance. She'll gladly listen to you and she'll grill you with a million questions until she's satisfied that she's squeezed and juiced every piece of information out of you.

PANDA FOR HIRE

Page of Swords is all about the student life! If you are currently going to school or you're considering going to school or taking classes or any kind – Bailey is the panda to take with you to accompany you through any of your academic ventures. She'll help you brainstorm, research and organize data and help you write the thesis of your essay. She hates doing citations, though – so do not try to persuade her to do that for you. Oh, and needless to say – she's also great with quizzes, tests and examinations. Upcoming chapter test? Bailey can rain down on that scantron with her eyes closed. Need to memorize new vocabulary? Bailey's got a photographic memory. Other than that, she's is always down whenever you need to learn about a new topic – and it doesn't need to be in a school or academic setting. She can help you sort out an ocean's worth of information to find a topic that interests you, or she can help you study deeper into a particular field if that is what you incline to do.

PANDA DISCLAIMER

Bailey is a curious little brainiac with a talent for learning and absorbing new knowledge. As mentioned earlier, she has the tendency to be a little snobby. Most of the time, it's because she's a confident panda who's not afraid to speak her mind.

Occasionally, though, she gets a little extra with just how much *she* knows that *you* don't know, and she may just get caught up with her "duty" to "educate the public". When she's running her mouth ceaselessly, she forgets the most important thing when it comes to learning and expanding one's understanding of the world, which is to *listen.* If that happens, make sure you gently tug at her ear to remind her to sit down and be humble. After all, if one only seeks to speak without any willingness to listen at all – well, might as well be talking to a wall by yourself, right? Or better yet, record your own voice so you can listen to it being played back to you.

Knight of Swords

I am Neo, the Knight of Swords, the Champion of Bamboos, the Prince of Air! Here I stand, and hear me roar – RAAAAAAAAAAAAAAA AAAAAAAAAAAAAAAAA!

Neo is an active and powerful agent of change. He tumbles at the intellectual and cultural forefront, challenging norms and traditions and bringing powerful ideas into the playing field to cause a tipping point to the collective consciousness. He's always asking questions: is it right? Is it fair? Is it wrong? Every day, he puts on his red cape and carries his sword with his bamboo emblem – for he is a panda burdened with glorious purpose. He speaks to spark change – and he speaks to be heard. He wants to seize the world by storm. He wants to start a revolution, a chain reaction of positive transformations. He cartwheels and dives – he articulates, and he demonstrates! And, at the end of the day – when he's finished his daily rounds of righting wrongs and dropping truth bombs – he relaxes his throat at the local karaoke, melting microphones and busting eardrums for fun.

PANDA FOR HIRE

Neo s is a proud champion of all that is right and good. He loves to experiment and express daring ideas in order to spark change and spread new thought. He is the panda to go to when you have a message you want to put out into the world, and when you are in need of activating your voice. He – *um. Neo? What are you doing here? Yes, I'm writing your section. Wait – what you are you – HEY*

I, Neo, the Knight of Swords, the Champion of Bamboos, and the Prince of Air have usurped the writing desk and gained control over this keyboard permanently – for I have an important message to impart. Wherever you are and whoever you are, join me! Scream at the top of your lungs and never apologize for who you are. Speak up for yourself. Speak, and demand to be heard. Speak, and let me hear you rooooAAR –

AND I, KIMBERLY MING TSAN, has regained *rightful* ownership of the writing desk, Sorry – what? *I'm not trying to censor you! There is a WORD LIMIT for – what do you mean this is an infringement to your freedom of speech? You literally have your mouth OPEN on the card!*

PANDA DISCLAIMER

As you can see, Neo can be overdramatic and incredibly intense when his ideas – instead of helping him conquer the world and create positive change - end up conquering him instead. He can be relentless and will completely disregard your boundary especially when – *ARRRRG! GIVE ME BACK MY CHAIR, YOU BRAT* –

I, Knight of Swords, have returned. At last, my space of written expression belongs to me. I need you to know that you are here for a reason. You have a message, an identity, a vision. And you are given a voice. Use it – and use it well. Use it to speak your truths. Use it to change the world. Use it to –

Queen of Swords

I respect you, which is why I will tell you exactly what I think. Truth may be hard to hear, but truth is liberating. Let it go. It is said and it is done. Look me in the eye – oh what these shades? Specially made for cool mama bears like me. No, you can't have them. You can admire them, however, but don't get too close. Yes, I love you with all of my heart, but a panda queen needs her space, thank you very much.

Queen of Swords will like to apologize on behalf of Knight of Swords – she had to grab him by the ear earlier so the author of this book could continue writing. Neo is currently being reprimanded by the Cool Mama Bear from the Air Kingdom – Valerie, and she only needs to cast a single look to bend him (or

SUIT OF SWORDS: THE AIR PANDAS   177

anyone, really) to her will. Indeed, Valerie speaks both with her silence and her words: she deploys her truth bombs and tough love with both diplomacy and grace, articulating her voice and message with conciseness, poignancy and elegance. And when she's not speaking, the weight of words impresses themselves upon her listeners before they are even spoken. She's the one panda that everybody fears a little, but also deeply respects and loves – because she will always treat you like an equal. Besides, it's not like you can hide from her penetrating and knowing gaze. She knows exactly what you're up to before you even open your mouth to speak. When this cool mama bear is not out taming the furry hurricane that is the Knight of Swords, she fences (verbally, and sometimes literally!) with her equally cool cub, training him and guiding him to think and speak for himself.

PANDA FOR HIRE

Valerie is not one to mince words or go on conversational roundabouts. She's an excellent panda to have around when you need to communicate something smoothly, clearly and fearlessly. She will help you say what you mean and mean what you say. She will also help you put your paw down when someone is trespassing into your space or throwing nonsense at your face. See the unsheathed sword swung across her shoulder? That's the stance she'll help you achieve if you enlist her help. She will make sure you walk with shoulders back and your chin held high – you'll be an untouchable panda.

PANDA DISCLAIMER

Oh, you'll definitely notice it when Queen of Swords is having an off day – this "cool" mama bear instantly turns into the "cold" mama bear. Losing her poise and her diplomatic grace, sharp words roll off her tongue, shooting into the air likes shuriken darts. Her words will cut you at the deepest places – not that she cares. She has a sword, and she is going to use it. With great power comes with great responsibility – which is why the Queen of Swords makes sure she never loses her cool. But on the rare occasion that she does, do not join her. You will surely regret it.

King of Swords

The more you know – the less you know.

A bear of supreme intellect, Sherlock Polmes is the guardian of the Air Kingdom and oversees all nerdy affairs. When he's not functioning as a walking encyclopedia or helping his fellow panda bears problem-solve their conundrums, you can find him at the ancient panda ruins, decoding the symbols and pandaglyphics and seeking to unravel the mysteries of an old emperor's tomb. Or, you may see him nose-deep into the challenging manuscripts of modern philosophy, trying to solve a paradox and piece together an argument that will settle the intellectual schisms once and for all. He does crosswords in pen and fumbles with a 10 x 10 Rubik's cube when he's bored and needs some casual stimulation of the mind. Needlessly to say, he cannot live without his coffee. He takes his coffee black – black and sugarless. Sharp and poignant like his mind.

PANDA FOR HIRE

Logical deducing, detail sequencing, patterning, decoding, deconstructing – Sherlock Polmes is your multi-functional panda computer and the answer to all of your problems. He never (and I mean never *ever*) loses track of his thoughts and he is always able to synthesize an ocean's worth of facts and information - presenting his conclusion and observations to you in simple, concise speech. If you challenge him to a chess game, be prepared to be brutally humiliated and savagely defeated. Basically – don't challenge him! But if you're humble and inquisitive, King of Swords may teach you a move or two. Makes sure you're truly ready to listen, though. His explanations and thorough breakdowns are bound to occupy the afternoon.

PANDA DISCLAIMER

An orderly panda of extreme details, King of Swords can be controlling, obsessive and unforgiving when things fall outside of his perceived pattern or when you challenge his mental domain with flailing emotions. He can become preachy, cold and unrelenting with his facts and he will not back down until one of you is on the floor apologizing or one of you dies. Ok, he's not that terrible because he's a panda at heart and he will never do something that extreme – but that's precisely the sentiment. If you are wise, you will occupy Sherlock Polmes with a task where he gets to utilize his mental talents so that he channels all his intellectual competence to good use.

SUIT OF CUPS

The Water Pandas

The Water Pandas cannot wait to meet you, to hold your hand, and to press their chest against yours and feel the vibrations of your heartbeat. They are affectionate and eternally loving, always wandering and sauntering about the Cosmic Garden. Always wide-eyed with butterflies resting on the tips of their noses and flower wreaths circling their foreheads. Right here, right now, as you read this passage - the Water Pandas invite you into their heart-space – a small but infinite place that heals all wounds and turns all sorrows into gratitude and joy.

Let your heart be an open field, a cosmic garden for you to wander and get lost in

While Fire Pandas are confidently owning their cuteness and Air Pandas have logically declared their adorableness – they perhaps still will never be able to compete with Water Pandas' naturally exuding aura of sweetness and cuteness overload. Like eternal children, they find beauty and wonderment in everything they see – always greeting the world with an open heart and unwavering love, and always ready to receive and give unconditionally, to feel deeply and absolutely, and to experience the subtleties, the textures as well as vivid colors that surround them and make life wonderful. Water Pandas want you to know that you should never lose connection to your inner child, your inner Water Panda – the part of you that yearns for color, for unconditional love, for the richness inside a simple moment. These bears know that it is easy for a human to think that their hearts or spirits can be broken – but that is not what hearts and spirits are made of. Our hearts and spirits are not made of fragile things that can shatter into pieces. A heart is an open space, an infinite field, a cosmic garden. A heart is made of love, and love cannot be broken or shattered. Love breathes and gives and heals and expands. That's what a heart is made of – that's what you are made of.

Love yourself, for you are lovely

Water Pandas adore you. They think you're adorable, because you are meant to be adored. They will never stop adoring you because they know what you're made of (love, of course) – the same stuff and fluff that they're made of. When you visit them, they will give you all the attention and devotion that they can muster. They want to listen to your story. They are keen to learn what you're thinking, what you're feeling, and what you're craving for dinner. They want to know you, to connect with you, to give you their trust. They will take you into their hearts completely, and they will never ask for anything in return. How wonderful it is that you exist – how amazing and breathtaking that you are who you are at this very moment. Water Pandas have a good nose for miracles and all things lovely, and they most definitely sniff it on you.

YOU CAN CALL ON THE WATER PANDAS FOR A SERIOUS ADORATION-SESSION IF YOU ARE:

- ☼ Looking to attract new friends, new family, new pandas and new romantic partners into your life
- ☼ Striving to be more open + loving & more appreciative of the connections around you
- ☼ Wanting to activate and channel your inner child for their pure joy, imagination and wonder
- ☼ Developing your psychic, telepathic and intuitive abilities – the Water Pandas are naturals!
- ☼ Wanting to explore and heal from your childhood experiences, conditionings and/or trauma
- ☼ Trying to overcome trust issues and paranoia, especially when it comes to people
- ☼ Looking to heal your wounds – from minor heart scrapes to deep spirit chasms

PONDERING PANDA

☼ What's something that is stopping you from being open to love, trust and the gifts of the Universe? What are you most afraid of?

☼ What does love mean to you? What do you consider gestures or signs of affection? What is your language of love and how has your inner understanding of what love is affected your relationships with yourself, with others and with the Universe?

☼ When is it "appropriate" to summon your inner child? Is there a time when you shouldn't tap into this archetype? Is it even "appropriate" to use the word "appropriate"?

☼ The wounds that we experienced during childhood or major life events tend to impact us deeply. They rewrite the way we relate to the world as well as the people around us. What are the wounds that you carry or have carried – and how are these wounds affecting the way you live your life now? How have they affected the way you experience your relationships now?

Activating Your Inner Water Panda: A Ritual for Some Serious Self-Love

Read and recite this passage for an instant Water Panda Power Boost – for the moments when you feel like you aren't enough, when you feel utterly unlovable, unsociable, and unsalvageable. Having those moments does not mean that you are an unconfident and unspiritual person. It simply means that you are in a moment in which you aren't so loving and kind towards yourself – and like all moments, it is a moment that passes.

An army of adorable water baby pandas approach you (you hear that? BABY pandas!) The pandas feel your soul trembling – it's quivering, dwindling, hurting. They sense it from you. They feel it and their hearts ache for you and they know that they must do something.

"Pandas – we must form a hug line! This human is falling out of love with themselves and THIS CANNOT HAPPEN!!!"

One by one, they line up before you, with one slightly larger panda (a teen panda!) directing them like a cute army sergeant. They come closer to you, and you bend down to pick up a panda cub – immediately, she extends her arm to give you a big, fluffy hug.

"I love you SO much!" she says with sparkling eyes. Another panda cub finds your leg and hugs it with all her might. "You're – the –

BEST!!" she squeezes you and shouts at the top of her lungs, using all her panda strength to banish the blues in your soul. Another baby panda grabs hold of your other leg and begins mock-punching it, chanting, "No more sadness! No more woes!"

One by one you are bombarded by cuddles and unconditional love. The pandas love you like a child loves their mother. They love you like butterflies and bees love a flower. They love you like the wind loves the sky and its freedom. They love you, a fellow child of the Universe, for you are so much more than you know.

Love yourself. For you are lovely. Adore yourself – because you're adorable. You really are. The Water Pandas want you to promise to never forget just how much love you carry in your existence – and how much love you deserve because, well, you're a being of love. How can you NOT be love, have love, know love???

They give you a solemn stare. You promise to always love yourself. You promise to let your heart stay open so love may pass and breathe through you. You solemnly promise.

And you mean it. After all, how can you lie to a bunch of cute cuddly baby pandas? Now that's just wrong!

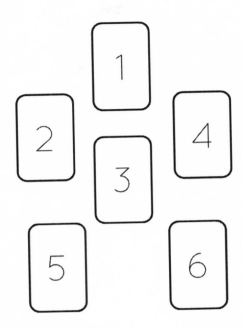

A Million Panda Hugs

When you feel rejected, wounded, and unloved – here is
a spread to remind you just how lovely and loveable you
are. Like you're so loveable, so adorable, so amazing – it's
totally insane to think otherwise.

1. **Entering the Cosmic Garden.** You are entering Water
   Panda's domain, a rippling dream-space with sweet currents
   of love passing through it always. What is stopping you
   from entering the space of trust and unconditional love?

2. **The Wounds that You Carry.** Often, we carry wounds
   that don't fully close – either from our childhood, our
   relationships or paradigm-shifting events throughout our

lives. What is a ghost wound that still lingers – a wound that reawakens and reopens itself when it's triggered?

3. **The Space that is Your Heart.** What is passing through your vibrations and your heart right now? What are you feeling – how do you feel at this very moment? If nothing is to block you from feeling what you're feeling, how would you feel?

4. **Barred Windows, Closed Doors & Locks.** What is the hidden "east wing" in the chambers of your heart? What is a place that you don't dare to touch, that you keep locked away? What are you most afraid of when it comes to love – what is your most vulnerable secret?

5. **A Million Panda Hugs.** Don't forget, the pandas looooove you. The Water Pandas are lining up to hug you now, and they have a message for you. Sit back and receive!

6. **More Hugs and General Adorableness.** Water Pandas are the best huggers, and they always hug to the fullest. It's too late for you to escape! You have no choice but to receive more love from the pandas. With this position, pull another card to receive words of healing and love from the Water Pandas.

Ace of Cups

I need a paw here – help me down from this oversized cup! Phew. I just put all of my love in it – and since you're here and you're looking so kind and amazing – you can have it! I may be small, but my heart is infinite!

Little Olive is the kingdom-famous adorable furball of love. She rolls and tumbles around daily to "hide" her panda affections here and there like Easter eggs for the rest of panda-kind (and mankind!) to find. She loves hiding her heart-energy in obvious places like, say, right in front of your face, in a cat's cuddle, or in a bouquet of flowers that lovers gift to each other, or inside a football that a father throws to his young son. She also places them in places that require a little bit of observation, coupled with the desire to receive – like in repeating angelic numbers on a smartphone screen, or tucked away beneath the rotten carpets of your soul layered and dusted with repressed negativity, long-term wounds and trauma (too much?) Anyway – the point is, this infinite little panda is *everywhere*, and that means love is everywhere. Love is a word, a gesture, a memory, an intention, a relationship, an experience. Love is what Little Olive is made of – and it is what you are made of.

CUTENESS OVERLOAD

Did you feel a tingle on your nose just now – as if it's just been brushed by a fluffy panda paw – ever so gently? That's Little Olive, saying hi to you. Did you also just feel like you've been hit by a waterfall on the head? Yup, that's also Little Olive dumping a bucket of feels, good vibes, healing and cosmic love onto your unsuspecting head. You didn't think Water Pandas are capable of pranks because they seemed so innocent, did you? Well, the Water Pandas are just as playful as the Fire Pandas – and their favourite thing to do is to overload you with cuteness and *awwwws!*

YOU'RE A SWEET, SWEET ANGEL

Each time we open our heart to a person, to a project, to a new idea, and/or to the world – we're always a little afraid that we may end up letting in some demons or shadow creatures that are not aligned with our highest good. If you are feeling like you are trembling with fear and mistrust at the sight of something approaching you from a distance or *wanting* something to approach you from a distance – Little Olive will like you to know that you're an angel from within and out. And she doesn't just mean that you are a good person. You're an angel – you are a being of light on Earth, you were born with wings on your back, and you are an image of purity and beauty and love. No demons, monsters or goblins can touch you from where you stand. It is your nature – inside and out. There's so much love for you – *so much love.* Allow yourself to receive it, because to have love pass through a being such as you is an absolute blessing and privilege.

Two of Cups

I see you. You see me. We are here for each other,
for all eternity. I'm yours, and you're mine. We
belong to each other forever, perfectly.

Many pandas mistake Kaia and Avery for a romantic couple, and they could be, I suppose – it was love at first sight in many ways. As soon as they saw each other, they knew they were meant to be together – because they know they are on the same wavelength, the same frequency, and their hearts saw each other so much faster than their naked eye ever could. Even if they didn't end up meeting that day, they would still be an iconic Two of Cups because it doesn't change the fact that they are from the same soul tribe. What brought them together was the deep knowing that they could trust each other, love each other and give to each other without worry and reserve – for they know their feelings will be reciprocated always. As they sit together, fur to fur, paw in paw, they know. If their lives were a movie, they would have the same instrumental background soundtracks (Ghibli-esque symphonies in triple time, and light piano on the side). If their relationship were a book, they would pick out the same font and the same color scheme. They recognize each other on a soul level – they truly *see* each other.

OTHERS SEE YOU WHEN YOU SEE YOURSELF

If there's something you've been eyeing to touch – a special someone, an opportunity to share your heart with the world, or a quest to find your tribe – Kaia and Avery have just the thing for you. They are placing the scarf of peonies around your neck, crossing it in the middle to create an infinity shape – leaving the other loop open for whatever or whoever it is that you have in mind. They seal their panda blessings as they clasp their paws over your hand gently. Two of Cups is all about finding yourself in the eyes of another – to create and form a connection, to match in frequency and heart energy. True connection can only happen when you have fostered this deep connection within yourself. Are you who you say you are? Do you trust yourself to be *you*, no matter what you say or what you do? When you see and recognize yourself for who you are and how you feel – that's when you are able to recognize yourself in others. That's when you are able to connect and resonate on a soul level.

WEAR YOUR HEART ON YOUR SLEEVE SO THE WORLD MAY SEE IT BEAT

You're holding the garland of peonies, folding it into an infinity sign – just like the Kaia and Avery did theirs. But you're afraid – you're afraid to share it. What if they don't want it? What if they don't want *you*? You find yourself asking these dark questions over and over, and then you look down to see that you never took the time to place the peonies around your deck. All this time…you weren't even wearing it. You weren't even sending out an invitation. You weren't even…open. You didn't think that you were worthy enough to wear it, to be seen in them, to actually invite someone to share that space with you. You didn't think that you mattered enough for somebody to step into your life, to see you for who you are. Well, you clearly didn't want to be seen, so you didn't put the garland on, and you didn't send out the invitation. Well Kaia and Avery are here – they are placing the garland around your neck now. Perhaps you would take it off again, and perhaps you would resist their efforts. But these Water Pandas are patient, and they are gentle. They will always help you wear it, and they will always be there for you.

Don't be afraid to wear your heart on your sleeve or in a certain way. Display it proudly. Allow others to see you and feel your heartbeats.

Three of Cups

We are different, yet we are the same. Each of us is unique, a different shade, a different texture, a different glimmer. Yet we are the same. We are black, and we are white, and we are pandas!

It took Juniper (hipster panda) and Darcy (dapper panda) an entire hour to convince the Sora (nerdy panda) to come out and play. He's an introvert, you see. His perfect day is simply a day at home, chewing and gnawing on bamboos and staring peacefully at the ceiling. But he loves his friends – and united by their mutual love for bamboo (and of course, each other), they gather at the fields. As Darcy and Juniper eagerly exchange frontline news of fashion trends in the Panda Kingdom, nerdy panda listens politely as he snacks on some leaves and waits for an opportunity to chime in (as soon as his friends touch on the topic of striped scarves, that is.) Together, the three pandas celebrate this moment of joy and belonging, their hearts colliding and merging into a mutual space of harmony and love.

YOU BELONG TO NO ONE, BUT YOU BELONG

You don't need other people to be happy – the pandas know that. You're independent, self-assured, and confident by yourself. You know who you are, and there is magic in knowing that you are full and complete. It brings about a special kind of joy when you begin to know someone else. When you see someone, recognize someone, love someone and honor someone, you are seeing, recognizing, loving and honoring yourself at the same time. Only with our own fullness are we able to celebrate the fullness in others. Only then does our love resonate and build. Only then do we expand into each other's presence, and make each other whole.

PANDAS ARE NOT SCARED OF REJECTION

The pandas know, however, that humans are very prone to this fear – and that we often feel powerless when pitted against its monstrously looming presence. When we do, we deny that we've ever needed another to begin with: *I'm fine. I'm fine on my own.* The pandas will like you to know that the presence of that fear is really an absence of love – an absence of love for yourself. You're afraid of that space in your heart, and you're afraid that nobody will deem that space worthy enough to walk into it to enjoy it. They will – if you do, and you're ready for company. You always are. Darcy is unfastening his bowtie (just his bowtie – calm down ladies) and he insists that you wear it – while Juniper is trying to size up your ear to see if his earring will fit. Sora approaches you to give you a hug. He knows *exactly* how you feel, but here he is, loved by his noisy friends. And just like his noisy, fashionable friends, he is loving you, nonstop. The pandas love you for who you are no matter what – and they are giving you all the love that their hearts can muster – which is a lot. Endless, in fact.

Four of Cups

My friend here won't stop drinking chamomile tea – even when he's tired of it. So I thought I'd made him some peach oolong to try, but how far out has this panda zoned!? Take the darn cup, you silly bear. The tea is getting cold.

Kit is yawning – his jaw is stiff and aching from inactivity. He's drunk all the tea on the table and yet he's still unable to figure out the conundrum before him – or is it behind him? To be honest, he doesn't really know. He doesn't know where this feeling is coming from. It feels like he wants something more in life, but he doesn't know what or why. Restlessly, he sits. He's bored of empty cups in front of him. He's bored of chamomile tea. He's bored of this wooden table, and he's bored of his furs.

"Take the drink," he hears an exasperated voice above his head. "My arm is getting sore." He looks up and sees the cup that is hovering. Or twitching, rather. His friend is really straining his muscles – or lack thereof – to keep the cup in place. "Oh! Sorry mate. Here I go."

GRAB THAT CUP. DRINK SOME TEA. TAKE A CHANCE!

If you're feeling bored – that's actually a good sign. I personally think boredom is the "cosmic itch", the Universal indicator that we are meant for more than what we are doing right now. When we yearn for something more fun to do, something more engaging, more worthwhile, more exciting – that means we are ready to expand, to go out and explore, and to try new things. The Water Pandas agree with me – especially the Four of Pandas. He's a bit of a dweller and an occasional moper – and it takes him a while to pick up the pace and act on his desires. But that's all good – that's just how he is. His friends know when to give him some space and when to poke his butt a little.

NO SHAME IN WAITING AND WALKING THE PANDA PACE

The pandas like to take their sweet panda time – unlike humans. We live in a fast-paced society that is constantly speeding and cutting to the chase. We rarely have proper time to mull over our thoughts and examine our feelings about something. If there is a nagging feeling at you, a feeling that you cannot name yet – take your time to get to know its voice. Maybe it's a small mundane detail, a scrambled code, a small emotional spasm, a passing cloud. But maybe it's a new story that you have never known. Maybe it's meant to lead you somewhere. Maybe it's telling you something that you need to know.

Five of Cups

There, there. You tried, and it broke your heart. But your heart cannot be broken. Your heart is a space where feelings pass through – feelings like this love right here, this love that I'm giving to you.

So Kit did end up trying that peach oolong tea. It was the most awful thing he had ever tasted, and his taste buds trembled in excruciating agony. Though this humble author will disagree on his tea preferences, it needs to be mentioned that Kit was brave to try something new. After his first much-dreaded taste-testing, Kit permanently vowed to never taste-test again. His friend, however, is comforting his furs with two more new drinks. After all, he just might find something that makes both his heart and his taste buds sing. He just has to keep trying – be it new tea, a new traveling destination, a new hobby, a new relationship, a new sense of self, or a new aspiration in life.

DISAPPOINTMENTS IN LIFE...THEY'RE STILL HERE, ARE THEY?

The pandas know that disappointment in life is all but normal. I know, I know – easy for a cuddly panda bear to lecture a human about sadness and disappointment! *Are you even capable of sadness because you're so darn cute?* The pandas are perfectly aware of their indomitable cuteness, so thank you for pointing that out. They will like to point out to *you* that if you're disappointed – that probably means you've dared to try or imagine something different. You took a risk. You stepped outside of your comfort zone. You braced yourself for impact – seeking joy, acceptance, excitement, inspiration – but ended up with disappointment in your lap. Oh, woe – but it's already been dealt. As it turned out, this wasn't what you wanted. But hey – at least you know what you *don't* want and you won't ever have to repeat it again!

GROW A BIGGER HEART

Some heartaches shake us with the intensity and magnitude of an earthquake – don't they? Those ones are hard. They make you feel small and inadequate, because your body isn't built to contain such pain. It was used to pain in doses – little jabs that make you bruise a little, or tiny cuts with flakes of skin and barely a trace of blood to show for. Not this time – not this heartache, not this storm that you're trying to weather. The pandas will like to let you know that you'll be just fine – even though right now, you're not. It's okay to feel broken once in a while. Those are the times when you mend and heal – when you remind yourself that you were whole before, and that you're going to be more whole than you've ever been...because the only way to outgrow your sorrows is to grow a bigger heart.

And here you are, a bigger heart. Buff. Soft, and tough.

Six of Cups

I'm wearing this hat with adorable cat ears, and it shall stay on my head forever - because it reminds me of you and your whiskers. Remember those days where we grew up together? - it makes my heart feel so light, light like a feather.

Every morning, before he heads out – Harry tugs his ears inside the cat-eared beanie, combing his head fur so the hat will sit perfectly on his head. By the cat-tail meadows, his best friend Ashe is waiting for him, grooming and cleaning his beautiful silver fur. When the cat sees Harry sauntering towards him, he meows in greeting and his tail begins to curl happily. These two have known each other for a long time, and they have shared many adventures together. Though one resides in Panda

Kingdom and the other in Felinia - the Kingdom of Cats, nothing can come between their friendship and the incredible trust and kindness they have for each other.

BE KIND TO ONE ANOTHER

Ashe was just a kitten when he met Harry. He was lost in the streets, hiding in a soggy cardboard fortress. Tiny but fierce, he snarled and scratched at anybody that appeared to challenge him – until Harry approached him, that was. This kind and gentlepanda had an energy about him that instantly calmed down the kitty's nerves. Though much, much bigger than the cat, Harry crouched as low as he could when he talked to Ashe. "You're gonna be okay," he said, and handed him a fish biscuit. Ashe took a bite of the fish biscuit and cried, for he never trusted anyone in his short kitty life, but he did now, and he trusted this panda with all of his beating heart.

A HEART CAN CHANGE

Life gets complicated sometimes. A lot of times. Don't forget to be kind to the people around you. Don't forget to be kind to yourself. Believe in the simple power of your loving-kindness and your giving. Trust that they will always, one way or another, find whoever they need to find. If you wake up one day with a vanilla ice-cream mood, you might have been visited by Harry and Ashe. They wander around the human realm during their spare time, spreading love and kindness and reuniting lost souls.

Seven of Cups

I thought I saw a white rabbit, so I chased after its bushy tail. But now I'm lost somewhere, and I could be anywhere, and perhaps nowhere – to be found.

Somni takes his panda naps leaning against his favourite rock – or rather, I should say that it's the rock that's been designated to him in order to quarantine his thunderous snoring. Napping has always been the favourite pastime for all residents in Panda Kingdom, and you can say that Somni is somewhat of a specialist when it comes to scheduled afternoon rests. As soon as he closes his eyes, he's off to distant dreamlands, exploring mountain ranges, ancient libraries and secret gardens. Occasionally, he stumbles across a hidden pit of snakes or a persistent ghost in a haunted castle. You can usually tell if its a good dream or a bad dream inside Somni's head. If it's a good dream, he snores. If it's a bad dream, he rapidly snores – you may even catch him doing some bed karate.

NOT ALL WHO WANDER ARE LOST

Dreams help us explore and unveil hidden treasures in our psyche. When we wander with a certain purpose, we allow ourselves to receive, to find, or to see something in a new light. Because we are always trying to bridge the gap between our imagination and our reality, a little uncertainty and curiosity can actually motivate us to follow the White Rabbit and turn the corner down to Wonderland. Sometimes our stories don't align, they don't make sense or things don't happen in a straight line – but that is the beauty of wandering. As we blur our vision a little and look beyond the stars we already know – as we search for pattern, a new constellation in the sky – what will we see? What will we find?

UNLESS YOU'RE REALLY LOST

Don't spend too much time daydreaming and checking out on reality. It's a pleasant place to be at times – I'm sure. Somni will probably argue the same thing since he sleeps all the time. But he's a panda – what's your excuse?

Eight of Cups

Panda opera voice: "Tiiiiime tooooooo say gooooodbyyyyye – "

During moments like this, Mei often finds herself standing a little taller. As her spirit towers over the mountain ranges, she marvels at the miniature landscapes, feeling the start of a thousand flutters inside her chest. What is it? Wings, emerging – transformed from the burdens that weighted her heart down, made her feel small and stuck and useless. But not anymore. As she waves her hand good-bye, the butterflies swarm and take off into the sky, her woes and sorrows released into the Universe's open embrace – lightening, brightening, turning back into love.

DECLUTTER YOUR HEART-SPACE

Mei is suave, savvy and fairly fast-paced for a panda – she doesn't like to waste time on things she no longer needs. As soon as something is no longer serving, she dumps it into the recycling bin. Some she would most certainly deem to be garbage and she often has to overcome the intense urge to annihilate it by setting it on fire, but she can never judge anything inside of her for being completely useless. There is no such thing as useless – things are useful and relevant for a time, and all of a sudden, they may not be anymore. It's hard to tell because there can be so much junk swimming in one's heart-space: an old boot from an ex, or floating barbed wires clinging to a self-damaging thought from a decade ago. They're mixed in with a myriad of gizmos and lost trinkets and wonderful memories that you are unwilling to part. But she's gotten pretty good at sorting out the items in her heart. As she turns her attention inward, she notices tiny whirlpools forming in the currents of her spirit, any strange places where water becomes heavy and deadened – that's when she goes fishing with her bamboo pikes. She has a pile of them by the foot of the mountain, by the way – in case you need to borrow them.

IT'S ALWAYS TIME TO SAY GOODBYE

Excuse yourself from the mess you're in – why do you need to explain yourself for saying no? Why does the world always need a reason for you to walk away? For wanting to leave? For needing space, needing growth, needing to go ahead, or needing to be alone? *Tell us why you won't stay with us.* Whose permission are you waiting for? The perfect time is now. If you need a gentle push, Mei will be happy to push you off a cliff to get you started on your flight.

Hmmm…that doesn't sound so right, does it…

Nine of Cups

Quite frankly, the Universe doesn't really know how to stop giving blessings. It's annoyingly eager and it's constantly enlisting the help of adorable pandas and other spirit helpers to send you all kinds of good stuff in life.

Every day, Gabriel polishes the golden cups and fills it to the brim with the water from the currents of the Universe – a steady, sparkling stream of never-ending joy, gratitude and love. Every day, they are distilled into physical form, and poured into the human space-time, into the dreaming souls that are wide open to receive. Every single day, Gabriel does this without fail, and before he pours those gifts into the world of humans, he makes sure he gives each cup a furry panda hug to charge it with the kind of affections and admiration that only a panda can give – then he releases it into mass consciousness to be picked up by those who are tuning in.

ALL THAT YOU ARE IS ALL THAT YOU WILL EVER HAVE

The majority of the human population doesn't believe that they are capable of receiving the kind of blessings they want. They don't think good things rain down from the sky every day, and many don't think that they are deserving of such gifts. So they forget to look, or they turn their gaze away so they won't be disappointed when the Universe is quiet. Gabriel is here to remind you that blessings *are* raining down on you every single day, nourishing you with its waters and freeing your soul from dust and debris. The eternal weather forecast on blessings is this: everything you can ever want exists. It exists in your precious life and all you need to do to find it. And when you do, oh – stars be glowing, treasures be unearthed, and wishes be coming true.

IF YOU ARE MEANT TO BREATHE JOY FOR JOY IS MEANT TO BE YOUR OXYGEN

...shouldn't you stop choking yourself with things that suffocate you?

Ten of Cups

I don't think you know just how eager the pandas were when the Universe asked them to look after the humans. If you ever see a triple rainbow – that's the pandas smiling from above. Either that, or someone spilled their rainbow hummus dip.

The Water Pandas gathered when the Universe summoned them for a meeting. Flowers blossomed with their panda footsteps, and butterflies tickled their ears with their wings. The Water Pandas listened carefully. The Universe asked them to carry its love and deliver it to the humans – for as much as they could and for as long as they could. The Water Pandas were ecstatic about the idea. They were happy that they were chosen, because they would have done the same even if the Universe didn't ask them. So they did. They carried love, and they carried joy. They carried blessings and gratitude and smiles and light. They snacked on bamboos when they were hungry, and they bear-hugged the souls of every human they met – squeezing the human spirit with all their panda might. They have been doing this ever since they started, and to this day, they continue to pass on their love to everyone they meet. And this will they always do, now and forever and ever.

YOU'RE A HAPPILY EVER AFTER. BECAUSE.

Look behind you – bet you didn't see the barrage of pandas lining themselves up in your space, didn't you? Pandas are gracefully clumsy, but they managed to sneak up on you this time! As you look over your shoulder, you notice that there is light wherever you look, and wherever you look, there is a panda standing there, waving at you. Pandas. Cute adorable lovely pandas everywhere! As far as the eyes can see! They're all coming toward you now – they are ready to pick you up, to celebrate you, to love you, to tell that they've heard the dreams you've dreamed of – to tell you that everything you have ever whispered under your breath or spoken out loud – everything that you have ever wished for – they are all coming true. The pandas are here to make sure of that. They are here to fulfill your wish, to let you know that you are loved, and that you are and will always be valid and wonderful and perfect.

THE PANDAS LOVE YOU NOW AND FOREVER

Seriously, they do. Now and forever. And ever.

Page of Cups

*There was a fish at the corner of the street – it was
winged and glistening blue. It glides on a dream
and needs no water to breathe. It whispers music
even though it's got no throat to sing!*

It must be said that there is simply no contest when it comes to
Page of Cups – or Jomie's - cute nose. This cute magical ball of
fur wanders around the Panda Kingdom with her best friend,
Sir Edward Fishington, a gallant knight fish with iridescent
scales that swims in streams of rainbows. Most pandas will cock
their heads towards the sides as Jomie strolls by, chatting and
chuckling to the seemingly empty cup that she's holding. You
see, not all pandas see what she sees, and many curious pandas

wonder what exactly is going on underneath that fuzzy beanie and inside that fluffy brain of hers. Many things hide in plain sight, away from the naked eye: secret doors, creatures lurking in between the folds of reality. Sometimes you just need to find the right angle to see what you need to see.

PANDA FOR HIRE

Jomie will say that she *feels* things rather than knowing them. The portals between spaces. The entrance to a timeless storybook forest. She doesn't know how she knows, but she just knows. She knows how to speak in a fairy's tongue, or sniff out long-lost relics humming with elven spellcraft. Invite Page of Cups to workshop the stories you're working on – she has a deep love for fairytales, fables or anything with a touch of fantasy. Invite her to play with your children, your real-world children and the child within you. Invite her to explore unknown spaces and daydreams with you – the two of you can get lost together, if only for a brief moment – away from logic and boredom. You never know what you will find when you're busy getting lost.

PANDA DISCLAIMER

If you are trying to get some adulting done, Page of Cups probably isn't the best panda to bring with you – unless you are okay with just babysitting her. She's a real sweetie-pie and all, but she's prone to getting herself stuck in the in-between-spaces, and she makes a big panda fuss if you don't have time to pay attention to her. Can't you see the fish in the corner, floating? What do you mean no? What do you mean now is not that *time?* It's always the time! Why can't the world just be the way she imagines it to be? Why does it have to be *different?* There's no reasoning with Jomie when she's sulking and flooded with gloom, and she's completely inconsolable when she refuses to see the world as it is.

Jomie is patiently waiting for her Hogwarts letter.

Knight of Cups

Follow the scent of a flower and you will surely find something beautiful. A dream, a wonderful riddle, a lazy sunny afternoon, or the warmth of someone's heart.

Prince Charles is the heartthrob bachelor in Panda Kingdom – his gentle, adorable charms have snatched many lady-panda hearts and caused numerable swoonings. Being the Knight of Cups, he always follows his heart and trusts that he will find joy, poetry and beauty. He's the kind of panda that slows down to smell the flowers by the road, picking a bouquet on the go and giving it to the next lucky panda that he sees, perhaps serenading a little if needs be. He loves doing things that make him happy, and he loves making his fellow pandas happy. And not just happy – to feel seen, and cherished. Ah! Every panda is just so lovely! How can he not tell them how lovely they are?

PANDA FOR HIRE

Call upon Prince Charles when you're in need of a little romance – romance with another beautiful soul or handsome being, romance with the pleasures in life, or romance with yourself. Show up every day with a little more love than you usually would – scoop your bowl of cereal with a big smile on your face. Tell someone you love them in unexpected ways. Sniff the ink and paper from fresh new books at your local bookstore. Pour a little more heart into everything that you do. Carry on your day with a happy sigh, even though it may feel a little cheesy. A little "excessive" joy can really soften and add colors to your reality. And let's face it – is there really such a thing as excessive joy? Knight of Cups winks.

PANDA DISCLAIMER

Okay, okay. Sometimes our Princes Charles can be a little too much of a walking rom-com. But hey! Who can blame this dreamy bear for dreaming? Sometimes he's not exactly practical, and the way he looks at you and talks to you – hmm. Is he even listening to you? Are you even on the same page? But he's so handsome, such an adorable bear – how can you resist? And he sings! Ahhhh. He's just so perfect. Who cares if he wasn't listening to me just moments ago? Who doesn't want to live in a storybook world where problems can be solved by a true love's kiss and convenient magic? Ahhh. The wonders of fairytale. Happily ever afters.

A QUICK NOTE
FROM THE AUTHOR

I fell for it again, didn't I!? Ugh! Charlies, stop being so adorable! You are distracting me from my writing! Stop. Stop looking at me like that! I am not going to fall for it again!

Too cute...must...resist...AH!

Queen of Cups

The space of my soul is the space of my love. You may enter it, and be healed by it. Share with me the stories of your past, your memories, and I will love you. And see you. No matter who and where you are.

When Penelope closes her eyes, she swims in a wondrous ocean of shapes, patterns and colors unseen by the naked eye. She reaches out to them, or most of the time – they come to her. These creatures in the water, messages in psychic bottles drifting in the currents, memories and feelings with gills and flippers that are lost at sea. This is not some hidden world, but it isn't easy to find. It takes a certain temperament, a certain stillness, a certain frequency and a certain heart to be able to access its entrance. Queen of Cups is no stranger to this land. She was born carrying parts of that world within herself, always connected to that fluid dimension – realities layered on top of each other, overlapping the lunarscapes of one's subconsciousness. Before you say it, Penelope knows. She knows what you're feeling. She knows what your wounds are and how they're hurting you. She knows why you're here, and why you are choking on words that you are dying to say. And she's here to uplift you, to heal you, to hold space for you – to free you from the claws and talons of your fears, so that you have room to save yourself.

PANDA FOR HIRE

You do not need to call on Penelope. She knows it before you do, and you will find her standing next to you, placing a furry gentle paw on your shoulder, at the moment when you decide that you need her. She's heard it with her heart way before you did, and she's here for you. Whenever you need a panda to hold space for you, to connect deeply, to commune with the language of the Universe – the language of love, Queen of Cups is here to hug you close. Sit and be in that space with her. Be in the space of love, joy, gratitude and healing. She needs nothing in return.

PANDA DISCLAIMER

Indeed, Penelope needs nothing in return. Your happiness is everything to her. As she opens herself up to hold your existence, to affirm you, to *see* you, she disappears into the currents of your emotions, your thoughts, your memories, your narratives. She grows so fond of hearing your stories, melting into the rise and fall of your words and forgetting to return.

Penelope – who was she? Who was she compared to the lovely creature in her arms right now?

A MESSAGE FROM THE QUEEN OF CUPS

Boundaries, my two-legged friend. Don't forget to live your life as your own. If you have a heart like mine, an open field with no walls and no boundaries – you need to build some fences. Nice ones, with a floral gate, and a fancy switch to shut the door when nasty things try to enter and poison your space. And by nasty things I really mean narcissists.

King of Cups

What a privilege it is to see you, to partake in your joy, to be loved by you. I am your humble servant. I promise to make the world a better place. For you, for us, for everyone on this earth.

One thing you need to know about Lawrence is that he loves his family. He'd wear a crown, for he is the King of Cups, but why wear a crown when you can wear a smile? The Water Pandas and pandas from the rest of the Panda Kingdom love him dearly – they can always feel him when he's around. They know the air is buzzing with love and the bamboo trees bend in humility and compassion – that the King of Cups is near. He cares about you – he will share with you his bamboos, a warm talk over home-made green tea served in his favourite blue mug, and call you his family. He is a panda of little words, but every strand of his fur speaks wisdom, speaks love. You will almost want to pick him up like an adorable plushie, but then you will remember how deeply respected and well-loved he is by the pandas all around him. You will maybe want to bow a little, but you will also remember that he doesn't care for bows – he just cares for your smile.

PANDA FOR HIRE

Joy is a funny thing. It is perhaps one of the only things on this earth that multiples and expands when you give it away. It's simple math, really. A concise science. A Universal Law, if you must. Lawrence, the King of Cups, is a panda with a simple vision: to make the world a better place, a more joyous place. A place where pandas and people and all creatures can grow and thrive. A world where peace and wisdom abound – a better world. The best world – heaven on Earth. Call on the King of Cups when you wish to serve, to cultivate and express your unique gifts in order to give to the world. He'll help you celebrate your existence and guide you to find others that are in need of your voice, your presence – who will in turn serve you and elevate your spirit.

PANDA DISCLAIMER

The world needs you. But the world does not need your saving. You can't save the world. The world has many stories – many tales that will touch you, change you, excite you, and even anger you – but not all of those stories are yours. You can only serve by telling your story, and living your story to the fullest. And when you're ready, you join your stories to the thousands and millions of stories that are told across the Universe. King of

Cups is now placing his paw on your head – gently, reassuringly, and carefully so he won't mess up your hair. He knows who you are. He knows you want to do good. And you already are. You exist – don't you? You're living and breathing – aren't you? And with that, you're already serving. Do good by making your story a good one. Don't worry about saving the world. Just *be* in existence. The existence that is you.

SUIT OF PENTACLES

The Earth Pandas

Earth Pandas are a practical bunch. They allocate their energy, time and resources carefully and are never wasteful. This is the main reason why they concentrate their efforts on the munching and crunching of bamboos - a very important task as a panda must acquire the necessary nutrients to sustain their jaws and enable more vigorous chewing. Stalks and leaves must be properly eaten and digested, which in turns vitalizes and nourishes crucial internal organs. Bamboos must be regularly consumed to amplify love, joy and prosperity in the body. As you can see, eating is a deliciously win-win situation and proves to be absolutely crucial to a panda's well-being.

Life is a glorious feast – a never-ending abundance of delicious bamboo stalks and juicy leaves

Why do Earth Pandas eat so much? You may ask – to which they will answer: why NOT eat so much? Why not eat until your heart is bursting with joy and gratitude? Why not eat until your belly is singing and orchestrating divine music that you've never heard before? When everything you've ever wanted is within your grasp – when everything you've ever needed is provided for you – why not eat your fill? Why not, indeed? The Earth Panda Kingdom is blessed with colossal bamboo harvests each year, and they give away their treasures freely to the neighbouring kingdoms because they know there is never a scarcity when it comes to the abundant resources that are available in the Realm of Pandas. There is never a need to worry. The Earth Pandas are always at ease and always happy, because they know their source of joy (bamboo) is never-ending. If it is never-ending – why worry? Why worry indeed?

Don't be fooled by the stalks that I got – it takes a conscientious panda to keep calm and panda!

Earth Pandas never waste time on limiting beliefs or emotional nonsense. Do bamboos make them happy? Yes, and they must consume them. Are there always enough to go around? Yes, so they will eat without reserve. If there isn't enough, well, is this something within their ability to change? Yes. Yes to all of those questions. Earth Pandas are very practical bears. You want to eat more? Eat more! You want more but you don't have enough? Get your butt in the field, then! Find a way to solve your problem. Manifest the reality that you want by exercising your competence. Stop hesitating. Stop complaining. Can you do it or not? If the answer is yes, why are you still here? Earth Pandas have a mantra: if you can't accept something, then you must change it. If you can't change something, then you must accept it.

YOU CAN CALL ON THE EARTH PANDAS FOR SOME HARDCORE MUNCHING IF YOU ARE:

☼ Hungry. Hungry for more in life – for more food, more abundance, and infinitely more joy!

☼ Craving for a little bit of luck, a tiny reward, a sign to show that you are on the right track and doing the right thing!

☼ Planning to cut the crap and get down to business. No more excuses!

☼ Working towards better health and relationship with food!

☼ Trying to be more productive and level up your organization, time-management and prioritization skills!

☼ Struggling with feelings of not having enough money, enough time, enough health, enough body image, enough anything

☼ Wanting to practice generosity and giving to overcome scarcity consciousness

☼ Wanting to tap into the universal flow of abundance

PONDERING PANDA

☼ What do you want to achieve in life? What can you do to get yourself there? When you picture yourself successful beyond your dreams – what will you have done to have gotten yourself there?

☼ What do you want to have more of in life? What's stopping you from getting more?

☼ What's something that you know you really should be doing? What are the typical excuses that you use to get out of things you should be doing – especially for yourself?

☼ In what areas of your life are you able to take more ownership and responsibility?

☼ What does it mean to have "more" in life? What do you value? How do you define "value"?

Activating Your Inner Earth Panda: A Prayer for Ultimate Abundance

Recite this ritual and visualize yourself partaking the story as you read along. Read this aloud whenever you feel like you don't have enough – when you feel like you're always making ends meet, and you're scared that you will never break free from the cycle of poverty that you are trapped in.

You are in a lush, bamboo forest, and you are here to make a wish. You are here to make a wish because you know your wish will be granted by the most sacred cosmic law. You're in luck. You always have been. You are in a constant stream of good fortunes. Sometimes those good fortunes come wrapped in sandpaper and they cut your hand. But you bleed out the toxins.

Sometimes those good fortunes hit you on the side of your head, and with a jolt of shock and pain you realize there is a heap of gold next to your feet.

And sometimes, those good fortunes are delivered to you in soft blankets and pretty flowers, scented like a perfect Sunday afternoon.

The Universe awaits. It has always been waiting for you – listening for your voice, for clues and whispered secrets to your happiness. Your name is written in the stars, your luck an undulating ocean of good, a sparkly treasure trove.

Whatever you wish for – that is of the highest good of all – will come true.

Whatever you wish for that is the practical resolution to your greatest joy will come true.

There's no delay. No excuse. No wasted time. No nonsense.

You deserve nothing less. You deserve everything. Everything now and everything more.

Everything you have ever had – everything you have now – and everything you can ever have.

The world is yours for the taking. Yours. All yours.

Here, Have a Fortune Cookie

When you feel like you need a stroke of luck, a wind of change, a sign of success, a gift from the abundance of the Universe.

1. **The Cookie Dumpling Cracks Open.** What blessing is seeking to break through to you – to enter your reality? What is on the verge of manifestation?

2. **The Paper Slip Carries a Message.** What is your lucky message? What does the Universe have in store for you?

3. **No, They Are Not Lottery Numbers.** Or are they? What's something you've never tried before? Something you have never done? What if you took that leap of faith? Put that golden intention forward? What would happen?

4. **You Munch and Crunch that Cookie.** There are many things you can be grateful for right now in your life. What tastes delicious and rich in your life right now? What's something that bring you the munch and the crunch – the joy of being alive – the joy of having what you have?

5. **What is Your Wish?** What do you want to have, to achieve, to manifest, to make real?

6. **For It Shall Come True.** Say the word. Cast the line. The spell is in the air now – let the Universe do its work. When your dreams come to you – how will you know?

Ace of Pentacles

Nom nom nom nom nom nom!

Luke is an excellent flutist. At the end of his performances, he bows, and he eats his flute, for it is made of bamboo and it has done its job. Occasionally, his untimely hunger may cause him to devour his instrument halfway through a modern rendition of a folky panda classic. This doesn't shock his audience, for they take that as a cue to munch on their own snacks. The munch and crunch of bamboos reverberate through the music hall – every panda enjoying a moment with their favourite food, eating and chewing without reserve. There's no convoluted rules or embarrassment – the earth pandas do what they want to do when it is time to do so. Pandas eat when they are hungry. A panda flutist eats his bamboo flute when he's hungry. When they're done, they give thanks to the Great Bamboo Harvest, and they eat some more.

ADMIT IT, YOU'RE HUNGRY AND YOU WANT FOOD

Admit it – you are hungry. Hungry for more, for treasures beyond your wildest dreams. Good. There's much to be had. The Universe has everything to offer you and all you need to do is to ask. The Universe will do anything to keep you fed and nourished – because that is what you deserve. An opportunity has fallen into your lap, the bamboo roots buried underneath your feet have reached maturity and they are about to burst forth with vitality and life. Here you are, and you can have anything and everything you've ever wanted. What are you going to do? Sit back and look constipated at this incredible cosmic buffet of abundance? Or perhaps you should be grabbing a plate, open your mouth and enjoy the feast?

STOP FUMBLING WITH YOUR FORKS

You thought about planting the seed. You considered the proper environment for it to grow, and ways to ensure adequate sunshine and nutrients to trickle into its stalks. You've thought it all – but here you are, still standing there. "Boo!" Luke screams at the top of his lungs and pokes at you with his flute. Did he scare you? Good. He wanted to. Now he's grabbing at your legs and attempting to bend you over onto his back so he can carry you. Carry you where? Well, that seed isn't going to plant itself. Time to get moving! Sorry – what's that? You want Luke to put you down now? You can take the steps yourself and this feels rather awkward? Oh, why didn't you just say so! Luke is putting you down now. You better get to work!

"CROUCHING PANDAS, HIDDEN BAMBOOS" - A SONGLIST
GIANT PANDA RECORDS

1. Over the Panda Rainbow

2. Bamboozling Dreams

3. The Moon Represents My Heart (Cover)

4. Munch the Crunch, I'm Busy with Lunch

5. The Sneezing Panda (Dubstep Flute)

6. Kiss Goodbye (Mountain Winds Remix)

7. New Year's Harvest ft. Pendrick Pamar

Two of Pentacles

One, two. We bite, and we chew. Together, forever,
we work this bamboo! Back, and forth. We flow,
and we groove!

Jazzy and Cruise are a team. Together, they've decided to tackle the toughest bamboo stalk in all of Panda Kingdom. Known as the Jawbreaker, the bamboo must be gnawed from both ends simultaneously with the same amount of strength and perfect synchronization. It requires two very precise pandas to execute this nearly impossible task, but Jazzy and Cruise are in the zone together. They do not need words to communicate rhythm — all they need is a look and a groove. Before long, Jawbreaker is evenly broken down and grew shorter and shorter towards the middle, and the two pandas have barely broken a sweat.

FIND YOUR RHYTHM
YOUR JOYBEATS

If you are hoping to take on the Jawbreaker challenge (the actual challenge or a figurative equivalent), you're in luck. Jazzy and Cruise are holding a workshop on productive flow and momentum down on Mapo Tofu Street. According to them, the trick is to munch to the beat of your favourite song – preferably a song that makes you happy and uplifted, or a melody that eases into your heart. The rhythm of joy and ease is the key to getting things rolling. Tune into your inner radio station and summon a piece of music of your choice. Then start moving your jaw and get chewing.

WHEN HARSH WALL NOISE & RADIO
STATIC IS PUNCTURING YOUR
EARDRUMS

What if nothing comes on when you tune into your inner radio station? What if there's no music in your heart? What if the volume button is broken and the noises are completely out of control? What if you can't find the right channel? What if you don't have a song? Take a deep breath – easy now. Don't worry. Moments of disconnection are perfectly normal and temporary. Jazzy and Cruise are here now – they've heard that you couldn't find your song to dance to. Before you find your "work music", they will sing for you. Or rather, Jazzy will sing for you – he's got a sweet throat and the voice of an R&B angel. Cruise beatboxes, and you should let him stick to his beatboxing because if he starts to sing – no panda in the Panda Kingdom can save you now.

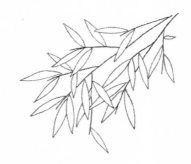

Three of Pentacles

Three pandas a charm.

Choco, Jasmine and Mica are members of an elite harvesting team in the Earth Kingdom. This incredible panda workforce is unparalleled in their efficiency, productivity and customer service and has over one thousand 5-star reviews on Panda Yelp. Choco is the leader and face of the group, overseeing general organization, administrative work, business growth, customer service and overall management. Jasmine is the muscle of the group, specializing in bamboo chopping paw-fu and her chi-induced air blasts can flatten acres of bamboo forests at once for maximum harvesting. Mica, talented in telekinesis and spatial decluttering, is in charge of transferring the fallen stalks and packing them into cargo boxes to be delivered to the rest of the panda kingdom. You see, each of them is excellent at what they do on their own, but the three of them need each other to excel as a team. Three pandas a charm!

PANEL, ENGINE, FUEL: A MACHINE RUNS LIKE CLOCKWORK

A machine is a sum of its parts – each tiny aspect of the machine has a function to fulfill. Choco knows that he's a control freak – I mean, uh, he likes to boss pandas around – okay, okay. He's an amazing leader and always knows what needs to be done; that's why he's the leader of the group. Jasmine and Mica each knows their place in the team and are always there to support each other. They are looking at you now – what are *you* good at? What are the skills and talents you can capitalize and showcase? How can you help others achieve their goals by being the best of yourself? How can you allow yourself to be supported by your peers and community to accomplish something you cannot accomplish on your own?

WE DON'T TALK ABOUT CHOCOPOCALYPSE

Choco isn't sure if his name chose his love of chocolate or the name chose him at birth because his love of chocolate was written in his soul-print. It is his blessing and his bane. Oh, there was an incident. We don't talk about that incident. Just know that Jasmine and Mica never dare to bring chocolate onto their job site – and they are careful to never attach an "L" sound to the end of Choco's name for fear of summoning the chocolate monster inside of him. It was a day of the reckoning – where Choco was driven mad by his desire for chocolate and he abandoned the harvest and went haywire, sabotaging the team effort and disrupting all that they had worked for. Without him, the team couldn't function and they could not complete the harvest. Jasmine did not know when to stop and had accidentally blown an unlucky passerby panda off the roads with her chi blasts. Mica did not know how much to pack and where he should deliver the goods. By the time Choco came to his senses - with chocolate chip cookie crumbs all over his face -   it was too late. Good thing the panda passerby didn't sue them – or worse, leave a 1-star review on their Panda Yelp page.

Four of Pentacles

This is my bottom line, my non-negotiables. No, you can't move them. Sorry. BeCAUSE! Things won't function if these pentacles are moved! I mean it. Stop touching them. Stoooop or I'll sit on you!

Every morning, Spartacus wakes up at 6AM, sharp. He brushes his teeth for exactly two minutes, and flosses diligently. He munches on a light snack, chewing meticulously to ensure proper digestion, and he rolls out his bamboo mat for panda pilates. He then goes through the rest of his morning routine before he tends to his field of bamboo bonzai's. The repeated tasks set the tone for his mood, which determines the productivity of any given day, and the productivity of every day accumulates into the success of a week, which gathers themselves into a month, then a quarter, then a year – so on and so forth. Indeed, Spartacus is very particular with his routines. If a system is proven to work, why change it?

A MACHINE THAT RUNS ITSELF

Spartacus' routines are the foundation of all his endeavours. He believes that the "machine of life" can only function at its maximum capacity when it's properly programmed – and the program must be maintained with conscientiousness and discipline. You may think this is contrary to a panda's nature to simply go with the flow – Spartacus doesn't think so. You can't go with the flow if you ain't got no flow. You can't operate the machine if the machine isn't up and running. To go with the flow, a panda needs to be healthy, a panda needs to be productive, and a panda needs to be at his best. Only then will he be able to do what his heart tells him to do, and have the energy to enjoy what he does.

DO YOU RUN THE MACHINE
OR DOES THE MACHINE RUN YOU?

As you can probably see, Spartacus is a little obsessed when it comes to routines. One day, his alarm clock unfortunately didn't wake him on time. As he scrambled to get off his bed, he tripped over his own foot and fell flat on his face. Angrily, he rose to make up for lost time and rushed through his flossing, and ended up damaging his sensitive gums with a cut. Having no time for panda pilates, he got dressed and headed out to the greenhouse to check his bonzai's. As he arrived at the entrance, he slapped his forehead as he remembered that he did not even have breakfast. To top it off, he could not find his bullet journal to schedule in tasks and pencil in data for his habit tracker. Driven mad by disorganization, he binged on fried bamboo chips and gained 2 pounds by the end of the day. "This is the worst day of my life," he wept pitifully as he covered his face with his paws. Thankfully, Mellon heard his cries of despair and came to his rescue. She carried her garden of Temperance with her, and as Spartacus sat next to her to share a Moment – he took a deep, nourishing breath and felt a steady wave of calmness wash over him, and he found his flow again.

Five of Pentacles

One way or another, the things we think we lost always find a way to return to us.

"Easy for you to say!" Peter stares at the broken pentacles on the ground, a mess in the cold, hard snow. They were once his treasured possession, but now they were gone. Stolen by the fates and forever taken from his grasp. Cursed with two left foot and clumsy coordination, Pete had tripped and without warning, the golden coins he was carrying slid out of his paws and landed on the ground with a loud clang. When he realized he had also dropped his bamboo snack (flavored with popcorn and premium cotton candy), he thought it must be the end of the world. He had nothing now – nothing!

ALWAYS MORE TO BE HAD

As he continues to sulk over his loss, Wenwen, his best friend, pats him on the shoulder – the remaining pentacles that Pete still carries gently knock and jingle against each other. Wenwen reminds Pete that nothing is lost forever, and that the Earth Kingdom remains forever abundant. Choco, Jasmine and Mica are working tirelessly every day to bring in more good fortunes for their tribe, Spartacus' bonsai plants are ready for trade next week, and if all else fails, there is always Luke's bamboo flute performances to be enjoyed. There is always more on the way, and more to be had. "You are never in lack," Wenwen says, her presence a furry hearth of steady light and warmth in the desperate winter storm. With that, Pete feels consoled, though he is still a little sad over the lost snack. He is grateful for his friend, who is always there for him during his time of need. She always knows exactly what to say to him to cheer him up.

THE ONE TIME PETE
GOT SLAPPED IN THE FACE

Wenwen is a warm, gentle soul while Pete is good-hearted but very worry-prone and melodramatic. One time, Wenwen found Pete in a heap of his own misery as he moped over the meals he had not eaten and the things he couldn't have. After failing many attempts to comfort him and distract him from his sullen moods – Wenwen was so frustrated that he slapped Pete across his sorry face. Pete, shocked and flabbergasted, looked at Wenwen's paw in admiration of her strength. "Wenwen," he cried. "I didn't know you worked out!" His friend shook her head. "That's enough, Pete. I get that you're upset, but you gotta stop complaining. What are you going to do about it? If you want more bamboos, go harvest some. Stop drowning yourself in your own tears." Pete wiped away his tears and nodded numbly, as he still couldn't get over the fact that the gentle Wenwen slapped him in the face. "This is stunning news," he grabbed her puffy arm. "Which gym do you go to?"

Six of Pentacles

I help you; you help me. Let's be best breads and
rise together in Grand Cosmic Oven.

It's a Sunday in the Panda Kingdom, and all the Earth Pandas know that if they head down Main Street and turn a corner on Cinnamon Alley, they will find Fred and Ginger setting up shop with their two sons, Billy and Bobby. As Fred stocks the tire stand with fresh homegrown bamboos and sugar canes, Ginger handpicks some of the greenest stalks to grind them into bamboo matcha for the tea-craving pandas that are guaranteed to saunter by later in the afternoon. The cubs are "helping", hugging and nibbling on the pentacles to "polish it" for display. They are handcrafted by Fred just the night before – he worked efficiently and elegantly, carving out the lines of the five-pointed star on mountain-copper and varnishing it with a secret herbal ointment to give it an extra shine. Well, not so secret since Fred always shares them openly – like Ginger, he publishes all of his DIY's on his Pandaterest board online for the rest of the kingdom to see and try. As generously as they share their recipes, however, nothing can compare to the authentic pawmade goods that they so artfully fashion – and their giveaway stand is always crowded with eager pandas that cannot wait to cherish their work.

TOGETHER WE ARE BREAD
WE RISE & TOUCH THE SKY

Walter always visits Fred and Ginger on Sundays. Before heading down to Cinnamon Alley, he wraps the blueberry and cream cheese bagels with a cream towel, tucking the freshly baked goods in with yet another layer of cloth. He places the bundle in a bamboo basket and he heads down to the giveaway stand. Fred and Ginger spot him from far away – Fred gives him a funny look, wiggling his nose and twitching his eye in an awkward manner – how they used to greet each other when they were schoolboys. Ginger flashes him a radiant smile and starts making her famous bamboo matcha tea – lots of cream, no sugar, and three-times stirred. The cubs tumble towards him in excitement, shouting "Uncle Walter! Uncle Walter!" as they attempt to wrestle him to the ground. It's always a delight when the families and friends meet and share with each other. Everything they give, they give from the heart – and on this wonderful Sunday, the panda hearts swell like a balloon, filling the air with joy and warmth.

GIVE & RECEIVE

Fred and Ginger always have something to give back to the world, for they know the world has been generous and kind to them and so it is only natural that they return the favor. They always give freely, help willingly, and receive gratefully. They do what they can to leave the world a better place than they found it. If you're feeling like there is nothing in your possession, your time or energy that you can spare – well, Fred and Ginger are here, but they are not here to pressure you into giving anything. Giving shouldn't be an obligation. Giving should be an act of joy. Giving can be simply saying *please*, and *thank you*, or letting the other person know, in whatever way, that you value them and you cherish their existence. Fred is handing you his handcrafted pentacle, customized to have your initials embedded along the edge. Ginger has a cutely stickered paper bag full of bamboo matcha for you. No, you don't need to give them anything in return. The only thing they need is that smile on your face. See, there it is. You brightened somebody's world today. Rejoice!

Seven of Pentacles

Treasures everywhere – in the palm of your hands,
in the corners of the world. What will you do, and
where will you go?

Sitting by the Pond of Wishes and Cosmic Doodads, Bobo slowly lowers the golden starry coin into the waters. He's reviewed his intentions, calculated the manifestation cycles and relaunched his grand panda plans to score the everlasting riches from the Universe. Indeed, the treasures of Panda Kingdom are always abundant, but what is the best way to get his paws on them? What does he want his collection to look like? How can he work with the resources he already has? Bobo is no idle panda, although he does appear that way most of the time – you know, just sitting there and cushionifying his butt. If you (dare) call him lazy, he will fling his straw hat at you like a deadly frisbee. Never too hard – he's not a meanie, gosh, no. But with just enough force to bamboozle you a little.

PATIENCE, TEA & GRASS JELLY

As you can probably tell, Bobo likes to fish. What will he find in the Pond of Wishes and Cosmic Doodads today? Sometimes, you find the wishes and doodads that you thought you were going to find. Sometimes you find them in a jiffy, and sometimes you find them after much sitting. Most of the time, those wishes and doodads find you instead – they find you staring into the pond, curious and wide-eyed, drawn to you by the line that you cast – the line that is connected to your heart. Whatever happens during Bobo's fishing endeavors, he always takes a sweet minute or two visualizing exactly what he will catch. Manifesting takes work, you know. And lots of preparation and careful planning.

IS YOUR BUTT SORE FROM SITTING?
DO SOME SPIRITUAL SQUATS

Bobo is not going to like this – but there was this one time he got too carried away with his grand panda plans that he actually fell asleep by the pond. It wasn't until much later that he snorted himself awake that he realized that he'd completely and utterly dozed off! What happened was this: he took stock of his lovely pentacles, decided that he wanted to try to fish for a blue one, and he sat down by the Pond of Wishes and Cosmic Doodads to carry out his plan. He got so caught up with lowering the pentacle bait in a certain way – *it must slice the water in this particular angle to generate triple ripples* – you could hear him say. *And I must hold the bamboo rod tilted towards the east – and then –* Before long, he was fast asleep from his over-planning and overthinking. When he woke up, he realized a whole manifestation cycle had gone by and he still hadn't begun to actualize his grand plans! So there you have it – even the most calculating and practically smart Bobo has his slip-ups. How about you? You can tell me later, because Bobo is coming my way and he looks like he is about to fling his hat at me. *This author must run!*

Eight of Pentacles

Stages cleared – level up. Bosses slain – level up. Skills obtained – level up. Level up, level up, and level up.

Matt Sheng is a hardcore gamifier – to him, life is like a video game where you constantly level up to become the best version of yourself. Practice makes perfect is his motto. In fact, if he weren't covered in fur, he would totally have that phrase tattooed on his lower back, right above his butt crack and bushy tail. Matt spends the majority of his day honing his craft – whether that is threading and hanging pentacles, prolonging his unblinking time in staring contests, or getting ready for the Hungry Bear Bamboo Eating Championship. He's always training and getting better at something. If he's not working, he feels an itch in his earth panda bones that he scratches by…you guessed it. Getting back to work.

NEVER STOP LEVELING UP

What are you striving towards – or what could you be striving towards? What are your unique "stats" as a "human character" in this amazing "game of life"? What makes you the hero of your own story and how can you capitalize on those skills? Matt will tell you that the skills that are really worth leveling up are the skills that you find hard to level up in a variety of ways. For example, the boss you're fighting at the end of a stage may give you a judgemental "so-last season" side-eye for the ripped jeans you're wearing, or the Universe may suddenly develop a wicked sense of humor and throw you a curveball and sends an invitation to all of your worst fears. Matt, a veteran level-upper, wants you to know that those hard levels are the most exciting stages in the game of life to beat because *they are the ones that drive and advance the plot*! Once you've "defeated the boss" or "rescued the princess" or "slain the monster guarding the treasure" – you will inevitably receive the upgrade that you need to move forward. You will – inevitably – level up!

STOP WITH THOSE SIDE QUESTS AND GET ON WITH THE STORY

Not ready to take on the "big boss" so you've settled with side quests that offer minimum experience points for leveling up and mediocre item drops? Well, maybe if you're a completionist and like to take life at a slower pace so you can explore all the corners of your map – if that's the case, fine. But *you* know what you're up to. Are you delaying your own story by avoiding the boss fight? Maybe you just want to feel ready, or maybe you don't know what to expect. But you will never know if you don't try! Are you not the one holding the controller? Well, if that's the case, press start and game on! Let's level up together!

Matt Sheng's favourite video games are Super Smash Brothers and Minecraft. When he's not owning noobs on his server, he's probably complaining about noobs on the server.

Nine of Pentacles

Pandas that hustle live under gold leaves that rustle.

Ever since Winnie started her online coaching business, she'd been traveling around the Panda Kingdom teaching her fellow bamboo lovers the secrets to growing lush bamboo gardens, improving growth stock as well as expanding acres. She believes in hard work, courage, resilience and strategy. "Any panda can be successful," she said during an interview for the Panda Times Magazine. "You just need to commit to your vision!" Having become a household name, the "Winning Winnie" is currently preparing to journey beyond the panda borders. Her first daring venture will be the neighbouring Kingdom of Cats and Woodland Bears – and then she plans to reach the animal spirits at the Golden Grass Terrain, boldly starting with the rhinos at Hard Rock and the skeptical giraffes at the Long Neck!

GET ON YOUR LEVEL - THE LEVEL THAT NOBODY CAN REACH

"Now - Matt from Eight of Pentacles has surely lectured you on the importance of leveling up," Winnie says. "If you don't level up to become the bigger and better version of yourself, how will your dreams ever be able to manifest and come true through you? If you're not strong enough, how are you able to be the vehicle to your destiny? Time to dig deep. You have a gift that nobody else can give. Me? I have a knack for growing delicious bamboos. That's my abundance that I'm able to give to the world. How about you? What are your inner treasures? The inner treasures, the everlasting creative flow that will never run out for as long as you live? What is the unique currency that only *you* have? See, you're already a million bucks. You just need to see that for yourself – then you'll be *rich!*"

RAH-RAH! HERE IS ANOTHER MOTIVATIONAL SPEECH

Nothing stops Winnie from delivering a life-changing and epically energizing motivational speech. She gave the same speech that you just read earlier at the Panda Ted Talk a while ago – by the way. The pandas in the audience loved it so much, they all curled up into a ball and started rolling around the stage in a flurry of excitement – it was a sight to behold. Winnie hopes that you realize that you can do anything you want in life. You can have anything you want – anything you can dream of and more. If you think your dreams are big and perhaps quite impossible – wait until you actually start pursuing them. They are going to get so much bigger when you realize the Universe will literally give you everything that you could have ever wanted. Everything and anything. For realz.

Ten of Pentacles

There comes a day when bamboos and dreams
abound, and there is enough abundance to go round
and round and round.

The pandas from Earth Kingdom are gathered at the Capital City – each bringing their treasures: lush bamboo stalks, shining pentacles strung together with lucky red ribbons, ingot dumplings made of pure gold. They surround their treasures, their hearts brimming with gratitude at the endless gifts that have been given to them. They give thanks to each other, to the beautiful harvests they've had throughout the year, to the delicious bamboo treats that they have been able to have every day, and they hug each community member to acknowledge their cherished existence. It is a special day, indeed. Together, they sing songs in reverence and celebration: this is how they have always been – abundant, and rich beyond measure. Together, they are a generous nation that never hesitates in giving, a group of adorable panda bears that have aspired since the beginning of time to grow and expand with each other – to elevate each other, and to multiply each other's treasures tenfold, hundredfold, thousandfold whenever they have the chance.

THE GIFT THAT KEEPS ON GIVING

One by one, the Earth Pandas approach you. It's a parade, a happy march, an invasion of blessings. Each panda carries a special gift that they shall place by your feet. It is yours, and yours forever. Everything you have ever dreamed of, the dreams and wishes that you carry on your person, your spirit, your history, your ancestral line, your lifetimes and soultimes – everything that you could have ever wished for with every single existence that you have ever had and experienced – are being realized, actualized, manifested, and made real at this very minute. You are a glowing river of abundance, a beacon of light that ships come home to. You are the centre of the Universe, a cosmic heartbeat in the flesh, a portal of infinite treasure.

BEHOLD, YOUR GLORIOUS EMPIRE

You would think that the Earth Pandas ought to run out of gifts and precious goods by now, but more pandas are making their way towards you as we speak. They smile and wave at you cheerfully – some are trying to feed you their hearty recipe of stir-fried bamboo, some are trying to show you the little handmade gems and trinkets shaped like toys for a fairy child. Some are trying to give you a hug, and some are simply giving you a compliment about what an amazing person you are – a wonderful existence to have been added to the cosmos. The Earth Pandas want you to know that it's been an absolute privilege knowing that you are here, in this point in time, in this precise cosmic location, in the very physical form that has made you *you*. What a delightful contribution to the Universe. What a glorious present you have been. Don't stop giving *you* to the world. The world deserves all of you, your anything, your everything – just like you deserve all of the world, and its anything, and its everything. You are abundance. Abundance forever.

Page of Pentacles

Crossing items off my to-do lists is almost as delicious as snacking on bamboo-dipped lollipops and herbal sugar canes.

Carefully, Pennie's shovel enters the soft, richly nourished soil. She begins digging, each scoop with practiced and meticulously measured strength as to not disturb the environment. Once she's finished the hole, she places the seed of the bamboo into the ground, surrounds it with fresh fertilizing particles and sprinkles it with high-quality water. It will take a couple of years for a bamboo to take root and ground itself to the earth, which may seem like a long wait to some – but Pennie does not mind. She is patient, and she knows that as long as she puts in the planning and hard work, success is always assured.

PANDA FOR HIRE

Unlike Page of Swords who likes to bury her nose in ink and paper – Page of Pentacles likes to get her paws dirty and learn by doing. What's the fun in learning if you're merely sitting in a classroom staring at a talking mouth and reading instruction manuals? No, she needs to feel something with her paws, sniff it to ascertain its value, and work it by experimenting with its physical properties. With the fluffy brains of a panda engineer, she loves to figure out how things work and how they can work better. Always seeking to improve her methods and fast-track productivity, she will be an excellent panda team member if you need her help to keep things organized, keep up with your scheduling and commitments, evaluate the pros and cons of a situation, and sort out the details of a plan in order to execute it perfectly.

PANDA DISCLAIMER

Page of Pentacles is supremely talented with planning, organizing, scheduling, bookkeeping, taking stock – she's a great administrative asset and you can count on her to keep your life together and grounded. Having that said, she has the tendency to get obsessed with planning. During such moments, she buries her existence into her bullet journals, scheduling apps, goal-setting to-do lists and completely forgets the importance of *taking action* in order to get closer to manifesting her goals. She can be quite the obsessive-compulsive secretary if you allow her to spiral to the point of no return – so be careful when you ask for her aid. Make sure you catch her in a balanced mood!

Knight of Pentacles

Werk, werk, werk, werk, werk!

At the bottom of a hill, Benjamin looks down on his smartwatch to track his miles: *a hundred and sixty-five rolls today – covering just over a mile.* It took him five minutes and thirty-two seconds to accomplish this task – which is twelve seconds faster than his previous record. He is delighted to conclude that his rolls have improved, feeling motivated to continue to crush his panda gym goals. Tomorrow, he will tackle ten bowls of bamboo salads and soup dumplings, aiming for fifteen bowls by the end of summer – followed by an hour-long practice session of posing and smiling cutely in front of the mirror. It takes hard work and dedication to maintain and excel at panda fitness, but alas! No pain, no gain. A panda must keep going to become the best version of himself!

PANDA FOR HIRE

Benjamin is one focused, determined and dedicated panda. Got goals to crush? Numbers to crunch? Milestones to hit? Knight of Pentacles is your panda. Need a life coach to kick your butt and motivate you to spring to action? Give Benjamin a megaphone and he'll push you until you are beating and fast sailing past your personal best. He'll help you measure your success and inspire you to compete in the fast lane. He'll help you achieve the numbers and stats and figures that you want by breaking down your big vision and map out the necessary steps that you need so you can get there. One step at a time. Every single step counts. Every micro-win is a valid, productive move towards the right direction and your ultimate victory.

PANDA DISCLAIMER

As motivated as Benjamin can be, he can be a little intense when it comes to hitting his goals and succeeding according to plan. The slightest misstep and screw-up can cause him to spasm and slam his face against the wall, blaming himself for his failures and lack of competence at executing a basic task. Not to mention to compensate for his perceived lack of progress, he plunges himself into perfectionism, workaholism and over-drive. If you've hired him to keep you on track with your goals, make sure you are also taking care of yourself and slowing down to acknowledge the work that you have done so you don't end up burning out and fainting on the hills (which has happened to Benjamin just one time – *OW! Who just chucked a pentacle at me? BEN! I am the AUTHOR and I can write whatever I want – how dare you disrespect my authority!*)

Queen of Pentacles

Will take care of you. Will also teach you how to take care of yourself. Now, don't just sit there with a vacant expression. Chop chop! Time to work!

Fierce and competent, Tamara is the boss mama bear of the Earth Kingdom. She is the practical mother to all – will feed you, sew up your ripped jeans, help you weed your garden and spot you during your bench presses. Her love has to be earned, however. Don't get me wrong - Tamara lives for the giving. She is generous with every single panda that she meets, but you know what's one thing she hates? Entitlement. If you're a lazy sack of a bum unwilling to take responsibility and own up to your life, what makes you think you can just sit there and get handouts from her? Queen of Pentacles loves pandas that loves themselves, and she only works for panda that also works for themselves. So get off your bumbums and start working!

PANDA FOR HIRE

Being the ultra-capable adulting queen – you can summon her help anytime you need to declutter the house, effectively speed through your shores, comprehend and complete your taxes, and/or stay on top of your daily hustle-bustle. Being a no-nonsense panda, Tamara doesn't like to waste time on whining or complaining. She simply gets to work and gets the work done. All about that practical love, Queen of Pentacles is also a firm believer in self-care. How can you function at your optimal if you're not nourishing your body with the proper fuel? Feed yourself. Treat yourself. Exercise yourself. Sleep on time every night. Take care of your body and your energy so your spirit can shine through that beautiful vessel. Last but not least, she will like me to mention that she is the absolute champion of DIY and she welcomes you to contact her if you need help starting your own Pandaterest board.

PANDA DISCLAIMER

As much as Tamara wiggles her nose distastefully at entitlement and lazy pandas – she is a giver at heart and she will work tirelessly for her loved ones – sometimes to her own detriment. If you find yourself trapped in endless chores and the daily grind, your inner Queen of Pentacles is probably on overdrive. Tamara loves her friends, her family, her community – and she especially loves her children. She will do anything for them. Anything. As she buries herself in task after task – mending her cub's trousers, picking him up from panda soccer and spending time with her husband's in-laws – she sometimes finds herself grunting at this thankless job of being a mother to all. As she fans herself late at night with an inked bamboo fan, resting her paws – she is reminded to take care of herself first the next day, and then she turns on the TV to watch some Desperate Panda Wives.

King of Pentacles

Colorful dreams and rainbow bamboos: this Earth Panda Papa will make all your wishes come true!

Octavius Pandam Maximus loves to look at "panda stock" – the flow of resources from one place to another, the currencies of abundance traveling the Panda Kingdom like a river of shooting stars…a river that continues to split and branch out until it submerges pandas everywhere with the energy of wealth, prosperity and ultimate fulfillment. One of his favourite things to do is to invest in young and aspiring dreamers that are seeking to manifest their vision into reality. He's the richest panda in Panda Kingdom, and he's never once said no to a request, a favor or even a loan. He needs nothing in return, because he knows abundance has a way of finding its way back to him. It is the Universal Panda Law.

PANDA FOR HIRE

King of Pentacles is your ideal go-to when you want to grow your business, your projects, or any of your life's ventures in exponential degrees. He knows the rules of manifestation and knows exactly how to ride the currents of abundance. True abundance is inherent in every panda, every spirit, and every human. To unlock your personal abundance, you must help another unlock theirs as well. The more you seek to give so that you and others may grow and expand together, the more wealth multiplies and piles up in your corner. With the help of Octavius Pandam Maximus, you will soar, grow, succeed and watch the world's riches pile and accumulate by your feet.

PANDA DISCLAIMER

On the very rare occasion (very, very, very rare indeed – Octavius will like me to stress) – King of Pentacles will, unfortunately, be temporarily blinded by greed. What can he say? When his stomach is growling in the wrong way on the wrong day, the disastrous urge to consume overtakes his generous and magnanimous panda spirit and he transforms into a hungry-eyed food machine – hoarding bamboos, slapping pandas that get in his way and whacking bystanders in their bums to ambush their bamboo stalks. He's not proud of such moments, but most pandas are able to relate to the blinding hunger he sometimes experiences, and usually warmheartedly forgives his transgressions. He usually gives all the bamboos back anyway, by barfing them out or ejecting them out of his rear end. Just kidding, that will be disgusting. You should have seen your face! He repays the pandas that he's eaten from with top quality bamboos from his own bamboo garden, and continues to give, share and invest to spread the energy of abundance.

The Panda Epilogue

Thank you so much for reading this book. From the very beginning, I knew this was going to be more than a guidebook. I wanted it to be special somehow - an authentic record and "guide" on how to walk the Way of the Panda.

I struggled to find the right tone, and the right way to introduce you to the lovely world of pandas. At first, I wanted these pages to have concise diction and intellectual flair, with practical tips on dissecting and analyzing the symbolism on the cards and how to integrate them with the archetypal meanings of tarot. Well, that didn't really work out. I was creatively constipated for weeks and could not produce anything of value.

Then, I tried writing this book as if it's a documentary to my creative process – a portal to my brain and how I visualized and concepted this deck from start to finish. That didn't work out either. I grew tired and bored of talking about myself and not enough about the pandas.

Then it occurred to me that the pandas had stories to tell. Each panda is a unique personality with a special message to give to the world. Each panda wants to partake in *your* story by interacting with you in profound or silly ways. They want to tell you what it's like and what it means to be a panda. They want to get to know you, to tease you, to have fun with you, to love you and at the end of the day, make your life a little (if not a lot) better.

The pandas were ready to tell their stories, and I just needed to listen and surrender my keyboard to them. So I did. I let the adorable pandas run amok on my pages and I hold space for their love to come through.

I hope that this book has been more than a guidebook to you - it is my ultimate wish to create something that is timeless and speaks to the soul. I hope that it's brought you warmth, joy, comfort and love. I hope that it's inspired you to move forward in life with courage and confidence. I hope that it's brought you closer to the dreams you are dreaming, and I hope that it's brought a smile on your face.

I wanted the pandas to be forever. I didn't just create a panda-themed deck to sell. I wanted to unleash a spiritual panda army – and now, these adorable panda healers and light-bringers that live inside a deck of tarot cards can now be held in the palm of your hand. I hope you treasure them – as they certainly treasure you.

From my heart to yours,
Kimberly M. Tsan

Notes